I

AM

THE

WORD

JEREMY P. TARCHER/PENGUIN

a member of Penguin Group (USA) Inc.

New York

I
AM
THE
WORD

A GUIDE TO THE CONSCIOUSNESS
OF MAN'S SELF IN A TRANSITIONING TIME

A Channeled Text

PAUL SELIG

JEREMY P. TARCHER/PENGUIN
Published by the Penguin Group
Penguin Group (USA) Inc., 375 Hudson Street, New York, New York 10014, USA • Penguin Group
(Canada), 90 Eglinton Avenue East, Suite 700, Toronto, Ontario M4P 2Y3, Canada (a division of
Pearson Penguin Canada Inc.) • Penguin Books Ltd, 80 Strand, London WC2R 0RL, England
Penguin Ireland, 25 St Stephen's Green, Dublin 2, Ireland (a division of Penguin Books Ltd) •
Penguin Group (Australia), 250 Camberwell Road, Camberwell, Victoria 3124, Australia
(a division of Pearson Australia Group Pty Ltd) • Penguin Books India Pvt Ltd, 11 Community
Centre, Panchsheel Park, New Delhi–110 017, India • Penguin Group (NZ), 67 Apollo Drive,
Rosedale, North Shore 0632, New Zealand (a division of Pearson New Zealand Ltd) •
Penguin Books (South Africa) (Pty) Ltd, 24 Sturdee Avenue, Rosebank,
Johannesburg 2196, South Africa

Penguin Books Ltd, Registered Offices: 80 Strand, London WC2R 0RL, England

Most Tarcher/Penguin books are available at special quantity discounts for bulk purchase for
sales promotions, premiums, fund-raising, and educational needs. Special books or book excerpts
also can be created to fit specific needs. For details, write Penguin Group (USA) Inc.
Special Markets, 375 Hudson Street, New York, NY 10014.

Library of Congress Cataloging-in-Publication Data

I am the word: a guide to the consciousness of man's self in a transitioning
time—a channeled text / Paul Selig.
p.   cm.
ISBN 978-1-58542-793-2
1. Spirit writings.   I. Selig, Paul.
BF1301.I18   2010   2010000612
133.9'3—dc22

Printed in the United States of America
15   17   19   20   18   16

Book design by Meighan Cavanaugh

CONTENTS

FOREWORD

A range of life events and choices, some purposeful, some seemingly random, brought me to the experience you are about to have as a reader of this book.

If I had not decided (rather casually, it has to be said) to reenter the world of college teaching by joining the faculty of a graduate writing program run by a small progressive college in Vermont, if I had not been curious enough to seek a psychic reading, for the first time in my life, from its program director, Paul Selig, and (as it slowly dawned on me that these readings delivered, far more accurately, the same kinds of transpersonal information that dreams do) if I had not continued to seek readings not so much for spiritual enlightenment (again, being strictly honest) but out of concern for maintaining my place in the world—if all these things had not come to pass, then I would not now have the pleasure of inviting you to share the adventure and the mystery of this book.

An adventure and a mystery. *I Am the Word* is both these things. It is also a spiritual teaching that promises, to those open to it, a special kind of reading experience on two levels of consciousness: as the mind takes in the printed words on the page, the whole person is being "worked on" at the level of pure energy—but only if the person wishes and permits it.

The exact nature of the teaching I leave to Paul's guides to lay out in the specific language in which they have chosen to deliver it. Let me simply say here that through a prologue, twelve chapters, and an epilogue, in a voice alternately urgent and loving, playful and serious, *I Am the Word* exhorts individuals to rise to a higher level of self-knowing and self-worth that in turn will help foster a radical shift in human consciousness in our planet.

I heard this book before I read it. Heard it over the phone an hour each morning for two and a half weeks as it was transmitted to Paul, 11:30 A.M. his time and 8:30 A.M. my time, from late February through early March 2009. I took notes as I listened, then read the transcripts that Paul typed up from his recordings. In slightly under three weeks of these hourly sessions a three-hundred-page transcript appeared that, with very minimal cuts and no additions, is the book you hold in your hands.

The process of dictation unfolded so quickly and so easily that the enormity of what was happening—completely coherent sentences, paragraphs, and chapters coming out of Paul far more rapidly than I could record by hand—became something taken for granted rather than marveled at.

Paul Selig is a gentle man in both senses of these words, a talented playwright and teacher who caretakes a little dog and oversees his two graduate programs with maternal solicitude and an impeccable sense of boundaries. As a channeler, Paul stands in an American tradition that, in the century just past, includes Edgar Cayce and Jane Roberts, but has older roots as well.

Paul will tell you in his own words how he "hears" his guides, but Chapter 6 describes the transmittal from their perspective:

> We are not speaking to Paul as if he is on a telephone. His physical ears are actually not even involved in this process. The thought is imprinted into him, and because he trusts our energies, he aligns to this and he is able to hear and repeat.

This description is strikingly similar to that given by the Swedish mystic Emanuel Swedenborg, who in the year 1745, at the age of fifty-seven, began hearing and conversing with entities he described as angels. "The speech of the angel or spirit flows first into our thought," he says in *Heaven and Its Wonders and Hell: From Things Heard and Seen*, "and then by an inner route into our organ of hearing so that it activates it from within." Swedenborg explains the process further:

> When angels talk with us, they turn toward us and unite with us; and one consequence of this union is that the two parties

have much the same thought processes . . . they enter into our whole memory so completely that it seems exactly as though they themselves know everything we know, including our languages.

In the same way, Paul's guides assert that the language and vocabulary they use is Paul's while the energy informing it remains something entirely outside him.

They also express concern about preserving the integrity of these words exactly as transmitted through Paul. The epilogue sets forth their wishes about editing (or more precisely, *not* editing) the text, which we carried out in a painstaking process of punctuating, proofing, and reproofing the oral transcript. Paul queried his guides about every suggested change or dropped word. In most cases, because this text is at heart an energy transmission, the guides wanted even ungrammatical syntax to stay intact, and we have observed their wishes. Their sometimes antiquated references—to Dictaphones, tapes, even steamships—remain intact. A few passages of personal material or outside interruptions were dropped with their approval.

As a witness and novice participant in the birthing of this book, I find on the surface that my feelings about it are sometimes complicated. The deeper I go, however—stumbling suddenly into realms of "joy joy joy joy joy," then stumbling out again—the simpler they get. Whoever or whatever they are, the self-described "collective energy" that informs these pages is by turns mystical, humane, ethical, optimistic, and above all, loving.

"We are all in this dance together," the guides tell us. "This dance, finally, is in its perfection and cannot be otherwise."

And so, reader—will you join the dance?

Blessings on this book and all who come upon it.

VICTORIA NELSON
July 28, 2009

PREFACE

During one of my weekly channeled groups my guides mentioned to one of the participants that I wouldn't really begin to believe the work that had been coming through me until I saw it written down. There was truth to that. When I "hear" as a channel, I generally hear in phrases with no idea where the larger thought will go, and I retain very little of the information afterward. I have described it in the past as being like reading fortune cookies, one after the other, with little sense of their connection.

The following week, I transcribed the recording of the channeling after my group had left, and was quite surprised that what had been delivered was a five-page lecture that required no editing. The information was coherent and wise, and the call seemed to be urgent: We were and had been anchoring in an energy that my guides called the Word.

The Word, as a frequency, is something that I have been working with, on and off, for fifteen years. When I first opened up as a clairaudient, I began to hear an insistent voice saying,

"Jerusalem Bible," and, eventually, I walked into a bookstore and asked if there was such a thing. It was handed to me by the bookseller and I took it home. I asked what was next, and was told to read *John* aloud and I did so, over the course of two nights. "In the beginning was the Word..."

I began transcribing the recordings of the weekly channelings in January 2009. A month later, I found myself unexpectedly released from a theater project I had been working on. Victoria Nelson, a colleague of mine, phoned me to tell me she had been reading the channeled postings on my blog and wondered if I might now be ready to write my own story, a memoir about how I evolved as a clairaudient. I was about to respond when my guides intruded into the conversation, saying that they had a book to write, a manifesto that would be completed in two weeks if we followed their instructions. They asked us to reconvene by telephone at an agreed-upon time two days later and they would begin.

I had no expectations, when we began these sessions, of what would transpire. In fact, every day I would sit with my dog beside me, a speakerphone in my lap and a CD recorder on the arm of the chair, and wonder if anything would happen at all. But my role as a channel has always been to show up and allow the information to unfold, and that is exactly what happened, chapter after chapter, day after day, until the text was complete.

In their epilogue to this book, the guides asked me to write a brief introduction to explain how I hear. When I channel, I feel the impression of the words form in my head, and it blocks out all other thoughts. As the words come, my lips move to form them, and I whisper them to myself and then repeat them aloud. Then the next thought, a sentence, or the fragment of a sentence, will be delivered and I will repeat that as well. Sometimes the information comes through at a lightning pace, other times more slowly, but the experience of it is generally the same: I feel a gentle pressure at my forehead, I am filled with words, and as I speak my body will often respond with accompanying gestures.

I am a conscious channel. I am aware of all that is happening but am somewhat receded. I take a step back and allow the information to come forward. I am often questioning the information that I receive as it comes, because I am very much a student of this work, and not the teacher.

What may be most significant about the work that I do is that when I channel, the energy that comes with it is tangible and can be physically experienced, not only by me, but by those I work with. My guides have promised that this will be the experience for those reading this book as well.

PAUL SELIG
August 2, 2009

The following are transcriptions of channeling sessions recorded in New York City between February 26, 2009, and March 14, 2009. Paul Selig served as the channel. Victoria Nelson was present via telephone from Berkeley, California.

INITIAL DISCUSSION

February 26, 2009

We want to talk about things. And we have chapters to write and we have issues to be absorbed in a larger text, twelve, fifteen chapters, each one about Christ and the mastery of that vibration in a being. Now we don't talk about personage of Christ as we do the personage of Victoria or Paul or Stanley or Fred. That's not really the issue here. The issue here is to discuss what it means to be aligned to a Christ vibration in a body that walks around and encounters other bodies in frequency.

Everything vibrates in a frequency. This much you both understand, and your readers will understand as well. Frequency is frequency. It's the molecular breakdown of the issue, as it were. Now Paul will back away whenever there is talk of science because he is frightened of it. He is not a scholar. However, we know what we talk about and when we say it's the basis, we simply mean that when you vibrate at a frequency, that is the frequency that you are aligned to, and when you are aligned to a frequency, that is what you call to you. That is your experience of yourself and you're experienced by others in this way as well.

So it's no big deal that you are in frequency. The question then becomes, what frequencies are available to you, and what do they mean? What does it mean to be in Christ at a certain frequency in tone, as it were? Paul is saying "tone," as in sound, and we will say yes, in an extended way, that is what we mean. Because tone implies resonance, and when something resonates, something is in alignment with itself and will call to it other tones, frequencies, expressions of the Christ that are vibrating at a similar level.

Now the Christ frequency, as it is understood now, is a high one and it has been misappropriated, entitled, by most people, who have assumed it to be a Christian basis in religion, and a religion, unfortunately, that has received alignment to the wrong-mindedness of men throughout time. And once you bypass the religion and you understand that the Christ is a consciousness, is a frequency, is an offering to man from the Creator to align to, then you begin to have a very different experience of understanding who you are. There can be no Christ in man without man's aligning to it. It is there as a silence until it is awakened, and when it is awakened it has one duty, which is to seek itself in realization.

No one is without the Christ. It has not bypassed anyone.

And there is, in form, a way to access this frequency that will be understood as we continue to transcribe our stories and our teachings to you both.

Now we do this with an intention, and the intention is that the recruitment to this service becomes larger than two people discussing an issue with guides' service in attendance. This becomes a larger issue in service because this is work that is meant to be understood by others, and in the time that it takes for us to be transcribing these notes and teachings and lessons we could be waking up a lot of people. So we are assuming now that this will be a vehicle to serve the awakening of others. We will assume this and we will work with you both to align to the possibility that restructuring the self in alignment with the Christ frequency is the work of the time, the work of the time, the work of the time.

Now we want to tell you some things before you go any further. This book will be twelve to fifteen chapters long. It will have a basis of understanding that is called something that will entitle each chapter. But that will not be the real chapter. The real chapter, in a funny way, will be a microcosm of a larger teaching. And once the small teaching is understood and inherited by the consciousness of the reader, then the work will take off in the cosmos, as it were. And the reader will begin to absorb structures beyond what has been read.

If you can understand that this is a process that we are intending, and it's as if many of the chapters are etched in

light and will be read in the higher frequencies once the key
has been placed in the lock by the reader, that is going to be
the process here. So it's as if we were to tell you "My Weekend
in Alaska" is the title of a chapter when, in fact, you would
gain an understanding of all that is cold by reading that chapter without knowing that that is what you are truly doing. You
would be resonating at a certain level that would allow the
Dictaphone to continue beyond what's served on the physical page.

So we will tell you this: Twelve to fifteen chapters, each
chapter has a title, each chapter is in service to a consciousness, to an awareness, to a vibration to begin the alignment of
the Christ in man in fruition.

Now this is no little deal. This is not *A Course in Miracles*.
This is not another book that has been written. This will be
transcribed by us through Paul. You will witness, you will
question at times, and you will direct when the Paul self pulls
out because he thinks this is crazy or because he doesn't want
to know the answers because they challenge his own belief
systems. So there is going to be a requirement for neutrality
for this process to take hold. Other than that, it's really a question of meeting and transcribing and owning the possibility
that the work that we are bringing forth is, in many ways, a
vehicle for the manifestation of the Christ in man.

When we talk about Christ, we will be clear now, we talk
about Christ as a creation of the God Self inhabiting man

in its fullness. We do not say, "You are Jesus" any more than we say you are a thing, or a that, or a light thing that can be called Jesus. Jesus is a personage of the Christ, a manifestation of the Christ in fullness, and there are others as well who have ascended to this level of understanding and frequency. And in part, their wisdom will be informing the text that we work with through Paul and through this process of understanding.

Tonight, you are both going to have an assignment in order to realize the book fully. And that is to imagine the book as sealed. A sealed book of promise that has been waiting to be unfolded for many, many, many years. And the unfoldment of the book will come in time. As each chapter is opened, the seal is broken, and the wonders that have been held within will open to the public who reads and wonders and accepts this vibration as its truth. Now this is the work of this night. Because once you understand that the book is already written and, to a large extent, this is a process of transcription and awareness and receptivity to the information held therein, it becomes a spontaneous act of being present for a miracle, as it were. Yes, indeed, we will say this: you can be present for a miracle.

Now to wonder what a miracle is is to ask yourself: What am I? What is the one before me? What is the sky? What is love? What is a tree? What is my name? You are a miracle. All these things are miracles. And what we are consigning to you is a miracle of understanding that will bring forth, in its way, the triumphant Christed Self into manifestation.

Now we do not say this lightly. This is not a tour book. This is not a how-to book. This is not a book that will solve your problems or take away the responsibility for your lives. That is very significant. Because when people buy books that are going to save them, they are paying someone to do the work for them, and, in fact, that is always a false truth, because the work can only be done by the self and the self's own worth is received in consciousness. So when the self does not believe it can be fixed, healed, responded to as Christ, you know well that that cannot be undertaken.

But in fact, those blemishes that stand in the way of the perfection of this realization can be cleared. And once they are cleared, the true face shines forth in beauty and wonder. And that will be the effect for those who engage in the process that we engage them in.

(Pause)

Transitioning now. And this is a transitioning time. And the time that you are standing in must first be understood in order for you to recognize the achievement of the Christ as it's stood until this time.

The manifestation of Christ in man has remained primarily an ideal for the last two thousand years. That has been the ideal that has not made itself fully known, fully realized, fully understood, although the teachings that would have enabled this to be so are present in every religion on this planet. However, the withstanding of that, the understanding that this is a time when these changes are remarkably apparent will become so understood by you that this will be a transition in your understanding of who and what you are, and who and what you have always been.

The time that you are standing in is a time of great change. And the change that we speak of is a cosmic one. And it is an interfacing with the consciousness of man and man's creations in a grand scale.

Step out, Paul. We need to give them more information and Paul is actually obscuring because he's trying to listen to what's being said as it's being said, and that's not an effective way to hear. The easiest way for Paul to do this is to step out of the picture as if he's in the bathroom outside the backyard and say, "Okay, there's stuff going on in the house and I trust what's going on in the house is safe so I might as well read a magazine."

So we'll say it this way: There is nothing going on in this body, Paul, that you don't have to fear being taken over by. There is nothing terrible happening. You can align to us and we will deliver the speech to the extent that you will step out. So this isn't a chapter, this is a discussion.

The first tape is for the book. This is not. This is preparation, and an understanding of how the work needs to happen. Now trials come to every man when he decides, "I am going to go forward and claim my consciousness as the Christ." Everybody you know of who has taken this one has had a hard time. So why, Paul, would you assume that your path, or the path of those that you teach, would be a whole lot different? It's not an easy path, and it's only not easy because it moves things. And when you unleash a cave by rolling away the boulder that has blocked its entrance, its face, and everything that had been sealed within comes out screaming as it's exposed to the light, that is the process you have undertaken. And those you work with, like it or not, have a similar experience.

Now it doesn't need to be hard. It doesn't need to be hard at all. It simply needs to be, and all that is hard is your attachment to the regulations you have placed on the self for the self to be and see and experience the world in a certain way. That's all there is to it.

If you don't believe that the trees will fall, when the trees fall you will be astonished. If you believe that trees fall all the time in the forest, you are not surprised at all when you find yourself stepping over tree trunks on the path in the woods. That's the way this is.

If you believe that the structures that you have created to give yourself worth, or prestige, or a feeling of safety, or a belief in your abilities to do certain things, if you believe that these are all permanent structures, you will be shocked when suddenly you are not able to write anymore, or when suddenly you have a new desire, or suddenly the prestige that you require to give you praise in an external way is vanished. Then what do you have?

Now if you know that trees fall all the time in the woods, you go, "Okay, here we go, I'm continuing on my path and I may have a tree to climb over but that's all there is to it." If you believe that trees never fall, and you are struck by a tree, you're gonna have a harder time with it, because your world will be rocked.

In this country, 9/11 did something very similar to the consciousness of this country. It realigned itself first to victimhood and then to outrage and then to a belief in retribution, and those were all required by the collective consciousness of the thinking and the experience of a country who did not believe that such a thing could happen to them.

If there had been another consciousness, the responses would have been fairly different, and the premonition of change, and the change in the status of this country, would have been worked with in a very different way. But because the country was in frightened action and then in revenge, which is always unconscious, because one cannot be truly conscious and be in revenge, you will understand that the course that was acted on, was approved of, by the mindset of a country that did not believe that a tree could fall in the woods.

There are trees falling all over the place right now, and people are climbing, and they're building tree houses and they're building tunnels. And people are hiding their money, and they're doing whatever they need to to prepare for difficulty, which, as you know, creates difficulty. You do not prepare for a divorce without planning a divorce, and you do not prepare for difficulty without planning for difficulty. That is different from saying, "I am going to save some money, I am not going to give up something that I need right now that gives me a feeling of safety." However, if you hold onto something for the safety that is going against the soul's requirements, you will find that there is a difficulty ahead. Because at this time on the planet's juncture, the realization of the soul's requirements must be put first. Period. It's going to happen anyway. All that will stand in the way is resistance.

Now we will tell you one thing. The country's role at this time is not to be the leader. It is to be the model of great transition. And how this country observes itself in transition will become the marker for the survival of this country in the passing years. This country has an opportunity now to relinquish power in a vibrational way that has been assertive and active, engaged "against" as opposed to "for." And once that is understood, that there can be a kindness and a consciousness and a wisdom, many, many, many things can change here. However, if you revert to the patterning of the past, which is the consciousness of the country as it still stands, of entitlement and outrage and self-congratulatory-ness for its own past conquerings, you will find that the country has a difficult, difficult time ahead of it.

Does this have to do with the Christ? Yes, yes, yes. Of course it does. We speak of the Christ in terms of consciousness, and the vibration of the Christ, which would bring about the change in consciousness we speak of to this country and to this plane of existence in a whole way, is part of the transition that we discuss with you today.

We're taking Paul farther out, so that we can channel directly. This will be an opportunity for him to stay in the background and look at a picture hanging on the wall so that we can get the words out without intrusiveness and questions. He has many questions too.

Whistler's Mother is hanging on the wall and Paul wonders what the big deal was. It wasn't a great picture, was it? However, what it was, quite simply, was an identity framed in consciousness, out-pictured and created and then witnessed by others, and that is everything in your life that you understand, experience, and see. So it is as worthy an issue, it is as worthy a painting, as anything else he might stare at while we have a discussion with the tape recorder and Victoria.

So we speak of the country and we speak of the Christ and we speak of the manifestation of the Christ in consciousness as we work forward to bring forth the required changes. We will speak of the book again and what the book needs to be.

It is a passage book. It is a book that you read, experience, and there is a passage entitled to its purchase. Which means, when you start the book here and you complete the book there, there is a different place, there is a different frequency, there is a different knowing on the other side. The book itself is the passage. If you think of the book as a steamship crossing a great ocean from one continent to the next and when you get off the boat you are on the new continent, that will be the instructions held therein. And by instructions we don't just mean what one needs to do to receive the Christ consciousness, but also the work that is done silently, through impressions onto the energy fields of the readers by the guides that are working with Paul and working with this on a global level to bring about this shift.

Paul is doing service in this way, regardless of what he thinks. And there are many others on the planet right now that are doing similar service, because this has to become amassed.

If you can imagine that these are temples being built, these are pyramids being built, and the high frequency at the top of the pyramids links to create a grid, a matrix of consciousness that will become apparent, an energetic system, a Christ vibration that will then be allowed to work through and inhabit and recreate itself through the personages, energy systems, beings of those who would welcome and embrace it, you will understand the mysticism and the practicality of this endeavor. So this will be one pyramid and there are many, many, many being built in the conscious intentions of the seekers on this plane at this time.

Now Paul has questions, and the questions are as such: "Will I be myself at the end of this journey?" "Will I still have my job?" "Will I still know what I want?" We have answered these in direct channelings and they will be answered again as part of the chapters of the book, but only in a way that will frame this experience for the new intelligence that is approaching this material for the first time.

Now Paul is going to be channeling daily for the next two weeks, whether you can be present or not. We are going to ask that someone be present to take the notes and to hear the voice as the chapters unfold. This is not like a book that is written over months and years. This is a book that is dictated, and it is in passage, so Paul will have to clear the decks a little bit in order to make this possible. He worries a lot that there will be nothing to say, that there is no chapter. It is easier to say, "There will be a chapter," than to fill one up. But if Paul listens carefully, he will realize that we have just written a pro- logue today, and an introduction that will suffice, with several edits, to stand as a whole chapter.

Now the passage that we speak of, of this book, of this tran- sition that the reader will attend to, is a transition of know- ing. And what people know when they finish the book will be different than what they know when they pick it off the shelf. However, we do not speak of knowing on an informational level, we speak of knowing in truth. "I know what I know what I know." We do not brainwash, we do not infiltrate, we create the opening for their own knowing to be made full within them. How would it feel, finally, to know? "I know myself. I know my worth. I know my love. I know my body. I know my path. And I know that I am deeply loved by my Creator."

Now Paul does not know this. He defends it by saying it's process, and that in time he will know if he's meant to know. But he has a huge investment still in anchoring all the reasons why the Creator could not love him, and others as well. "Because I am this, because I am that, because I don't do this, because I do that." All of this is an excuse and a way for the ego to prevent the self from releasing its power to the Creator. When you are in the Creator's love, you are one with who you are in truth, and all of the things that embellish the self, that keep the self separate through embellishment, which means, "I am this, I am that," all of those false tokens one hangs on their shoulders as reasons why they are separate from God's love, or others' love, or the self's love, all of those things must be cleared.

Now you will do this, Paul, as others do it. But we will use you as an example through the book as a way to see the self as healed. We will use Victoria to the extent that she is present for these channelings and we will use descriptions of others as well who you don't know or you do know, simply to say, "an example of someone who does this, that, or the other thing that needs to change in order to realize herself as the Christed Self she truly is."

But other than that, you will be understanding things on a level that is global. It is global, this work, but the global is realized through the individual and that has always been the case. When there are enough people, frequency, at present, vibrating at a certain level, the change will be significant and will be felt, and will resound in a wonderful song.

So we thank you both this morning for your attentions to our thoughts and we will give you the title of the book now, to the extent that Paul can stand away: *I Am the Word: A Guide to the Consciousness of Man's Self in a Transitioning Time.*

"Word I am Word through this intention to realize this book in its wholeness, in its accuracy and in its wisdom. I am a clear channel for the transmissions that are to come forth in wholeness. Word I am Word through this intention. Word I am Word. Word I am Word."

Thank you both and goodnight.

PROLOGUE:
IN THE BEGINNING

February 27, 2009

We're ready for this. And this is a call to action. And we say a call to action because the docile nature of your being would prefer you stay asleep, but this is no longer available to you. The times have changed and the time for recognition of yourself as a Divine Being has come. Period.

Once you understand that on a higher level your frequency is one with your Creator, everything seems to change. Once you understand that the availability of this energy that we will call the Christ is available to you, to all, everything changes. Once you understand that the Son-ship, your Son of God Self, is who you truly are, everything changes. If you are aware of this already on a minor level, you can get an understanding that the heavens are about to open to you. When you have an understanding that this is the time of this coming age of Christdom, everything changes. When you believe that you are one with the Christ, everything is changed.

Now we ask you questions now. Why did you come here? Why did you come to this land to incarnate in a body and to be realized as a person? Why did you come? Why did you come? Why did you come? This is the question for today. Why do you come back into a body and have experience that will move you this way and that, upwards and downwards, and through a lifetime? Why did you do it? Why do you come? Now we will tell you, and we will tell you very simply. Why you have come is to realize yourself as the Christed Self that you were intended to be. That is the mission of man. That is the mission of every man. That is the mission that you have been bequeathed and that you are answering to, each one of you, in your way, as you transpire to move through this time.

Now no one is without this promise: That the Christed Self will become realized within you to the extent that you align to its vibration. That is the promise. How does this happen? How does the Christ manifest itself in man? How does one come to become himself as Christ? That is the mission of this book. That is the action of this book. And that is the teaching in this book that we will give to you.

Those of you who have come to this place of reading are already aware that the times are significant, and that which you have believed to be true is falling away as veils fall away from the clouds. Now we will say to you this. When the veils fall away, what is revealed, finally, is truth. And when truth is revealed, the recognition of it comes quickly and you will begin to understand through the process of experiencing this book that what you are is the Christ embodying himself as man. That is the job. That is the teaching. And that is why you have come here to this reading and to this experience of yourself as Christ.

Now many of you are going to ask, "What does this mean? What am I then? What does it mean to be the Christ?" And we will tell you very simply: what it means to be the Christ is to be in the frequency of Christ, and to recognize the self in its divinity as one with the Creator without the separation of self that the ego process would keep in place to diminish the glory of the self as one with its Creator.

Now once you understand that the Christ is, in essence, the vibration of God as realized in man, and that it can be recognized and awakened and made manifest, you will begin to believe that everything is possible in this world. But you will understand that the possibility of this begins within you. Period.

You are the safety of this action. You are the one who chooses it. You are the one who allows for it, and you are the one who believes it can be true. To the extent that you align to this energy that we deem the Christ is the extent to which you become aligned to your own self in your glory. And once this has transpired, your frequency has adjusted itself to a high vibration when all things are resonant with God.

Now when we say this, we are not speaking metaphorically.

We are not giving you a symbol. And we are not giving you a lie. We are not going to tell you that a man can become Christ, in truth, if that is not the case. In fact, the lie is that you are not Christ, and it has always been the lie. You have been given permission to realize the self in fullness. You have been given permission to self-identify as the Christ. And you have been given permission to realize that this can be so.

We have given it to you. It has been given to you by others. The message of the Christ teaching was this in completeness and it has been regarded as something other, and as parable, for far too long. The understanding of the self as the Christ brings to it the Christ. And once the Christ is merged with the soul that it is created in, miracles occur.

Paul is asking, "Where is the Christ in me? How do I identify this part of me that you speak of?" And we will tell you now. The Christ within you is a frequency that is aligned within the heart center and it glows like a flame and it brings to it that vibration and frequency that co-resonates with it. And that which it brings to co-resonance is the Creator. If you understand that your light is a piece of the great light, then you have the beginning of the understanding of your Christed Self. If you understand that this light, in its blooming, in its flame, in its action, is the action of the Christ within man, you have a deeper understanding. If you begin to understand that the action of this Christ, once and for all, is to become realized as man in completeness, then you have the mystery of the Christ revealed to you. And the mystery of the Christ, and how it shall be revealed, will be the causation of the action of this text.

We bring it to you slowly now because Paul will have to transcribe these notes, and also we are finding that the slower transmission of energy aligns to him so that he does not get caught up in the language to the extent that he has in the past. And when the language comes slowly, he disregards the larger thought and becomes a more pure channel for the words that emit through him.

Now we talk through Paul today as a collective, as a collective energy that has come to this plane to manifest the Christ in man. To awaken those who are called to service to bring forth the Christ frequency in all that is. The Christ frequency is dormant in most men, but it is as if the radio station is still playing, and the receiver needs to be tuned. And once the receiver is tuned, all men begin to play the same music, and the music is beautiful.

We do not speak of a loss of individuality. We speak of truth, and the resonance of truth. If you can speak, Paul, of what will come, we will teach you as we teach the readers of this book.

We will speak now to what it means to become the Christ in frequency. It means that you align to a frequency, to a vibratory frequency, that is higher than the physical realm, and that is higher than the emotional realm, and that is higher than the mental planes. It is a high frequency. It is the causal frequency. And the frequency that it emits is one of high frequency that brings to it the Christ. You become that which you intend, and you cannot be that which you are not. Period.

When you become the Christ, the seed that has been planted has grown into fruition. The Christ is the seed of God within all men, and its awakening at this time is the job, it is the action, it is the requirement, it is the message, and it is the truth of all men. It is what is for this time. Period.

We now want you to know something, and we want you to know that Paul is being taken out more deeply than he is used to, because this will align to the energies that need to come through. And it will feel strange to him. And you will have to bring him back if he starts to drift, but this is a new experience in frequency for him as well. He is used to mandating what the energy feels like when he speaks with us, and that has been a process for him of growing comfortable with our energies. But when we speak as a group, and we are coming as a group now, we are actually coming at a very, very high pitch, which we then need to align to his frequency in order to be heard. So we speak differently with him and we are moving him out a little bit so that we can become responsive to the requirements of this teaching.

You are wondering what we are? Where we come from? What our mission is?

We are the Ascended Masters and we come through

different names, and we have been present on this plane for thousands of years in different forms. We are the great teachers. We are the missionaries. And we have a great love for mankind that is deeper than you can imagine. And as we teach you, we approve. And as we teach you, we pray that the love that we experience for you will be met with your recognition of our love. We give you praise for your experiences on this plane until today.

BUT TODAY IS THE BEGINNING OF A NEW JOURNEY, and we are here to teach you. We are here to speak with you. We are here to give you the understanding that you will require to speak, to believe, to be truly what you are in truth.

Now we want you to know something: that this is the moment in the history of man where man has an opportunity to become one with his soul's destiny. And we don't speak of this on an individual level. We speak of this on a collective level. And we speak of this truly as the response to the Creator within man that sees itself realized in form. What this means, Paul, is that this is the time of resurrection. This is the time of the resurrection of the Christ. The Christ mission has always been to be risen in man. And that has been impeded by a lot of things, some of which we will speak of, and the predominant obstruction to this action has been the frequency of fear, and the fear that has encased this planet for so long is actually being removed. And the removal of the fear that encases the planet that acts on each of you as a bad tape will leave, but not without a little bit of a fight.

Now on an individual level, this becomes experienced as change, and self-identification with those things that have frightened you, because everything makes itself known as it relieves itself and transforms. Everything makes itself known on its way out, once and for all. On an individual level, the changes are vast and we will work with the individuals here, as we can, through this teaching, on a higher level.

This is happening on a planetary scale, and the matrix of fear, as removed, will align this planet to a blessing, to a creation of light that will transform everything on it. This is the time of this promise.

However, it is also the time of change. And it is the time of choice. And as choices are made, the trajectory of individual destiny and planetary change are made manifest. So we speak to you now with great love when we say: If you don't get this right, you're going to have a difficult time, not just as an individual, but as a planet. If you don't move forward in the Christ vibration, if you don't wake up, wake up, wake up to your own Christ Self in form, which of course requires you to witness the Christ in everything and everyone, if you don't wake up, we will have a hard time and you will as well. And not because of anything bad, but because the choices that will have been made through fear will have their repercussions.

So yes, we will say that we are taking an action here to avert crisis. But we will say to you this: This is the promise of this time, that the Christ will be made manifest in man. And this teaching, each day, will show you how this is done and bring you to a place where your frequency can align to this truth.

Now ask yourself this: Am I willing, at this time, to engage myself fully in a process of transformation that may require me to release beliefs that I have held to be true? Am I willing now to engage in a process that will ask me to recognize my fear and to absolve it from its path by releasing it completely to the Christ? Am I willing now to be on a path of radical change that will leave me naked and resplendent in my frequency and without the tethers to a past self that are no longer serving me? Am I willing now to go on a journey with the Christ of realizing myself as the child of God made manifest that I am intended to be?

If you say, "Yes," to this, we will encourage you to read forward. If you say, "Yes," to this, we will work with you now. Because we are in frequency, we can work with you where you are, and the resonance of this book will actually be beyond the pages, but will be instilled in the frequency of the words and the intention that this book has been created in.

So each of you, if you are now willing to receive, we would like to bring the energies to you that will make this so.

We ask each one present, in their own space, to begin to realign the self to the possibility that the body that they are standing in is actually a vehicle for the consciousness to experience itself through and that the matter of the body can be transformed as energy. If you understand at this moment that you are a body frequency, that your body is ashift in frequency as we work with you, you will begin to feel the energies come through.

Now we ask you each to begin to receive energy in through the seventh chakra at the top of the head. And we ask this energy to go through the body to align each center, each chakra, each energy vortex in the body, to the higher frequency in preparation for the journey to come. And this will happen simply. You allow this, please. There is nothing else for you to do at this time but align to this frequency through your intention to receive it.

Now we are going to work on you individually, where you are, at this time, at the time of your reading. This is the time of the summoning of the frequency. So we ask you now to receive light in through the third eye, to awaken the mind, to awaken the sixth chakra, to awaken the self to your intention of purpose, and once this intention of purpose is set, then the rest of the work can resume.

We offer you now this honesty: We will work with you, align to you, and rework that which needs to be reworked for your highest good to the extent that you align to the willingness to be in a transformative process. This will happen now. If you say "Yes," we will work. And we will open to you as you open to us. We come in love, we come with direction, and we come with an encouraging word. What you will experience on the other side of this shift will be unlike anything you have experienced in your lives. This is the promise of the Christ: to be in the heavens while being on this plane. This is the promise of this time.

I Am Word. I Am Word. I Am Word.

Thank you for this. This will be the end of our prologue. So be it.

ONE

THE WORD

February 28, 2009

Let's talk about things as they are. By what they are, we mean, what things are today, in the current state of your consciousness. There are things in your life that you wish were gone. There are problems that you've created which dismantle the ideals that you would like to live by. There are feelings that you contend with that make you feel terrible. All of this is the state that you walk around in. And we want to rectify this today. And the way to do it is to first understand that anything you experience you choose. And you choose it in two different ways. You choose it on a level of consciousness, which means you intend to get something, or you choose it through your unconscious behavior and belief systems, which means, "It always happens to me and I don't know why."

Now both of these things are operating concurrently, so you always have a combination of things going on: your life as you intend it and your life as you undermine it through your unconscious patternings. And the two things fight all the time. "I want a lover, why don't I have a lover?" "I want more money, I can't seem to keep more money." "I want a friend, but I don't have a friend." You can ask all these questions and we will give you the same answer anytime: that when you have a pattern that sabotages your own life's intentions, you have unconscious patterning that needs to be cleared. Now this is one level of understanding and we will say that this is number one.

NUMBER TWO IS QUITE DIFFERENT AND IT ACTUALLY has to do with consciousness on a larger level, on a global level, on a level of matrix.

You all are in agreement about many things. You all are in agreement that pigs can't fly, and that's appropriate. Pigs can't fly. However, you are also in agreement about things that don't withstand the laws of gravity. And these are things like, "I am not allowed to know myself as a Divine Being." "Only the priest can give me the release of my sins." "Only the father in heaven can solve this problem, this is not for me."

Those are three examples of ways that you hold larger patterns of thinking; we will give you many more. We will say to you this. The belief that civilization has been here for so many thousands of years is a collective belief on this planet.

It is a collective belief because the evidence you have found to date supports it. So you go into agreement with it and that becomes your reality. If you believe that there is only one dimension of experience that you can access, and that is the belief that you share, guess what, everybody? That becomes your experience. If you believe that you can shift and move between dimensions, and that becomes a reality in a way that can be proven and experienced, everybody suddenly will say, "Oh yes, we can move within dimensions." But in order to get to that place of consciousness, the matrix of belief, the system of belief that has withheld consciousness, must be contended with directly.

So the problem is this. You say you want the spiritual growth, you say you want the alignment with the Christ, but the ceiling keeps hitting you in the head each time you try to go higher. And the ceiling is the belief systems that you have held, that others have held, that you hold as a community and as a people about what can be possible. So if we ask you this, "What would happen if there was no ceiling?" what would your response be? "There has to be a ceiling. I have to know what the limits are. I have to know what the rules are in order to play the game with myself." Do you understand this?

Well, there is a ceiling, there is always a ceiling, but the ceiling changes as you align to it and go higher. As you outgrow your clothing, you don't expect that clothing to fit you. You expect to require new clothing. Well, you have to require the ceiling to get higher and higher and higher as you ascend in frequency.

When you ascend in frequency, your vibration lifts. As your vibration lifts, the requirements for your growth transform themselves and then you are presented with new opportunities to align to the next level of consciousness, and so it goes, up and up. You do not grow from infancy into adulthood overnight, nor do you grow into your Christed Self, the self that knows the truth about your own divinity in fullness, in one quick reading of a book.

However, what we will tell you now may surprise you. The beginning of it is the hard part. The understanding that you are the Christ and that it can be made manifest is the key. Once the key is in the lock, the door is open and you are on the run, because the energetic configurations that are required to bring this into form can be brought to you with your intention to require it. If you say to somebody, "I only want a big house with a big lawn," the realtor is not going to show you the studio apartments. They are going to say, "This is what you requested, I will bring it to you." If you say to the universe, "I want to manifest myself as my own Divine Being, as my Christed Self, as my Higher Self embodied," however you want to decree it, you have to understand that you set in motion a process and once this process is begun, this process continues. You may pause. You may break. You may wander away and you may wander back, but the evolution of your soul cannot stop itself from forward motion and your soul already knows that this is the key to your growth.

So we will say to you this: Once the key is in the lock and you have said, "Yes, I am on this journey," your own soul will manifest itself and the opportunities you require to bring this growth into achievement will present themselves one day at a time. Now the manifestation of the Christ is not a little thing. It is not as if you get a new hairdo. It is not as if you change your clothing and then walk around in a robe and make people feel better. That is not the point at all. To be the Christ simply means to be yourself in full realization of your power as a piece of God in action.

"In the beginning was the Word and the Word was with God and the Word was God. He was with God in the beginning."

This is the decree. You are Word. You are an aspect of God being brought forth into light. As you journey, as you access this information, you become Christed in consciousness. When you become Christed in consciousness, you ascend. When you ascend, your vibrational frequency elevates and aligns in new patterns that cannot hold the old, and the old falls away as you rise. When you rise, your landscape changes. How it feels to see the world, how it feels to see the self from a higher vibration, is markedly different from what you can imagine. Because you understand your role as an aspect of the Creator, you move forward rapidly to bring to you the mandates of your soul's choice. When you are in your soul's choice, you achieve that which is required for your soul's achievement. It cannot go any other way.

So we say to you that the process that you are choosing has consequences, and the consequences will make themselves known, and they will also be your pride, your fear, your loathing of the self and the body releasing in ways that will become apparent. Because these are the low frequencies that must disband, that must release, that must go away for good. If you are to light the balloon, the sandbags that keep you tethered are those things of lower frequency that cannot go for the ride.

Now you have investment in these things that control you. They keep you safe, they keep you dormant, they keep you in the illusion of separation. "How can there be a God that loves me if I feel such pain?" "How can I be in a war with my fellow man and still be in God?" "How can I know myself as good when I secretly believe I am bad, or I am failed, or I am unloved by man?" These creations, self-loathing, fear, war, are all creations that must be cleaned from the self as the self ascends. How this process happens will become part of this book. In subsequent chapters we will address in detail how one goes about taking out the laundry, as it were, and how one goes about releasing the past in a way that will liberate the present.

How one does this through ascension is different than how

one does this in daily life. When one is in ascension, one is rising and the tethers are releasing and the past self is being discarded as the new self incarnates in the body you are in. The new self, the Christed Self, is incarnating in the body you are in. The old self walks away and does not come back, because the old self was never truly there. It was always illusion that you were separate from God. It was always illusion that you were not loved by your fellow man. It was always illusion that there was war.

Now we are not discounting physical experience. Physical experience is very real. And you turn on the television and there is famine and there is war and there are all these "strifes" that preclude people from believing that such things, the things that we speak about, can be so. But we will tell you this. On one dimension, these things exist and they are teachers, if you will learn from them and they will release. On a higher level, we say they are illusion because the physical reality that you exist in is illusion as well.

Does that sound like a cop-out to Paul, who is questioning us behind the window? We will say no. As you begin to understand your own ascension, you will begin to understand that those creations within and without that you have contended with have been manifested by you individually or collectively, and can be released, individually and collectively. One man cannot war with his fellow and that brings peace, and that

peace will resonate. One man can ascend into his Christ consciousness and change the world. And this has been done on
a singular level many times in this history of this plane. It is
going to be done now in many, many, many, many people as
the planet begins its ascension into the new millennium of
peace and understanding and truth. That has been the promise. It is the promise. And those illusions that will continue to
present themselves, the self-loathing, the fear, the war, may
continue in a lower frequency for those who require it, but it
will not be the case as you ascend in consciousness. We said
earlier the view changes, everything changes, everything is
changed.

Now when you invest in the self on a daily basis, and you
walk around saying, "I'm gonna work through my stuff," or
"I'm gonna talk to my friend," or "I'm gonna go to the doctor and discuss my problems," you are working through stuff.
You are talking to your friend and you are talking to your
doctor about your problems. But that is not ascension. That is
a process, and a beneficial one, of healing the emotional body
on a day-to-day level. While you may lighten the load and
while you may transform your consciousness through those
actions, they are actually very different from aligning to the
Christ consciousness and going on the ride of your life.

Now everybody, guess what, is on this ride at this time. No
one can be away from it. However, the degree of understanding

that you receive from your own self about what is happening, why it is happening, what is going forth, will change everything as you contend with the manifestations of your own Christed Self embodying as you.

Guess what, everybody? This is the time. This is the time. This is the time. And the wake-up call has been heralded, and this is an aspect, this treatise is an aspect of a creation that is happening on a global level in different vocabularies, in different treatises, in different ways to speak to people about what they need to do to bring forth their manifestation in the Divine Self.

Paul, right now, who was raised with no religion at all, has acclimated to a vocabulary that we work with with him because it resonates culturally and it signifies great truth. The same truth can be told in a mystical vocabulary that would reach people who did not believe that Christ was so. Because there have been many Christs. There have been many teachers. There have been many who have ascended and are way-showers. And every religion holds these people in regard, because they resonate. And the resonance of them has created structures.

Now the structures of religion, we wish to say, are only beneficial to the extent that they hold thought in productive ways. And there has been a way to hold thought through organized religion that has been beneficial to man. But true religion, if you can understand it, is a belief system. Everyone has a religion. Everyone does. Even the atheist has his religion.

Now organized religion, in its current form, has become blaspheme to many, because it holds within it hatred, "idiocracy," fear, and control. To liberate the soul means one needs to be free of fear, and any religion that dictates a fear-based doctrine of hell or damnation cannot liberate a soul. One will never leave the house when one is told what is outside the house can kill them. And if that is a lie, there would be many people living indoors without knowing the sunlight. So, everybody, guess what? If you release at this time, at this juncture, any belief that the journey that you are about to go on will imply your blasphemy and your fear of damnation to be incurred, we say to you, "It Ain't Gonna Happen."

This is about freedom now. This is about peace. This is about love. And how can you not have love in God? How can there be a religion that would hold anyone outside of itself and call itself God? The outrage of this in the higher dimensions is *out loud*. We are outraged *out loud* by the misfortune of man to create for himself damnation where there was meant to be love. We are saddened by the role the higher teachings have played in imprisoning and slaughtering innocents. We are heartbroken at the magnitude of pain that man has endured in the name of God when God would not bring pain. He cannot bring pain. He is love made manifest.

Now God allows man to create his world. God gives man

permission to speak his truth. And you can hear His truth or you can hear the truth of your buddy Fred, who says, "If you don't do it this way, you're gonna be stuck," or "You will be punished," or "Bad things will happen." It's much more convenient to stay tried and true to the voice that says to you, "Be afraid," because that is the voice you have honored in your spiritual growth since the beginning of time.

You have believed you have been separated from the Christ, and to the extent that that has been so you have created a world that exists in separation. Now that that is being released, the structures that have been created to keep man from God in fear, in misalignment, are being shaken to the core and the tumbling down of the walls will make a great sound. But it is a sound that brings forth liberation and light. When the wall has obscured the light, no matter how beautiful the wall looks, the wall must be razed, and we are razing the wall individually, in collective groups, on a race level through your consciousness and through this process of ascension.

The Word is the vibration of God in action. Word is action. It is creation. When we say to you, "I Am Word," we are decreeing ourselves as the Creator in action. When you decree, "I Am Word," you summon to you your own anchoring as the Christed Self and begin to make this manifest in form. The journey of how to become this energy in a way that you can feel, receive, understand, accept, believe, inhabit in truth is what we are intending for you. This is the freedom of the time. This is the freedom of the time. This is the freedom of the time.

To take a journey now simply means to say to yourself, "I am going elsewhere. What I believe to be true may not be true as I enter the different landscape. What I believed I needed to carry with me on this journey may not be required, so I will hold my suitcases very lightly and be willing to divest myself of that which is not needed as the journey progresses. I will believe that I am being led on this journey, and that I do not need to be fearful of where I am being directed because I trust that my soul is in charge. I can believe right now that this is a journey for good, and that this passage will be unlike anything I have believed I would encounter. But as I go, I will have the experience that is intended for me, for my own soul's journey has its own requirements, and I will see the landscape before me that will reflect back my own needs."

(Pause)

"Let each one know themselves as Light." This is the decree of the Creator at this time. This is decree and this is the heralding of the new dawn. So get ready, everyone. This will be your call.

We want to give you an informational session about what you can expect as you go through the process, through the reading of this book, and, one step at a time, we will take you through the industry needed to shift your consciousness and to align to the Christ vibration. Some of it will be through thought. Some of this will be through intention of thought and through actions that you will be required to take in your physical lives to bring forth the changes that we speak of. But on a more magnificent level, it will happen to you through energies that we will be bringing forth through the reading of the book and through the exercises herein.

We will stop right now with this information:

To become realized as your Christed Self will require you to believe that you are loved. If you will believe now that this is so, even for an instant, we will begin to bring forth the energy of the Creator through you to align you to this love.

"I AM WORD THROUGH MY BODY." THIS IS THE INI-tial decree to bring the body into alignment with the vibration of the Creator. "I am Word through my body. Word I am Word." When you affirm, "Word I am Word," you give to yourself the Word vibration as Self in manifestation and you bring about a process, an alchemical process, that aligns your frequency to the vibration of Word.

"I am Word through my knowing" very simply says, "I am Word through my consciousness." We will also say to you, "I am Word through my consciousness" intends you to understand that "I Am Word" signifies itself *as* consciousness.

And so consequently your consciousness frequency becomes Word, or the Creator in consciousness. "I am Word through my understanding of myself." "I am Word through my belief systems." "I am Word through all that I know to be true." All of these affirmations herald information implanting into your energy field that will then realign your energy field to the Christ frequency and to the frequency of the Word.

Here are the steps we take to attune people to the frequency of the Word:

1. I am Word through my being. Word I am Word.
2. I am Word through my vibration. Word I am Word.
3. I am Word through my knowing of myself as Word. Word I am Word.

What these steps do is actually incur change in the organism that you are, body, mind, spirit, and the evocation "I am Word" commands the change on the level of particle response, so that your entire frequency, physical and consciousness in form, will begin to realign itself to the frequency of God.

As this is molded, you are transformed into the image and likeness of your Creator. This is done first in the level of the causal body in the auric field. The energy field begins to transform itself down into the physical form that can hold this frequency when it is ready. The body cannot hold this frequency when the body is dense, and so consequently there will be a purging, of sorts, of those things that create density. And these are the things we alluded to earlier: your fear, your rage, your shame, whatever needs to clear, and, frankly, whatever is an impediment to this growth will end up releasing as well. You can only pour so much clean water into a glass without having the residue finally rise to the top and release. You are the glass, the water is the light, it is consciousness and the residue is that which is not the light. Very, very simply put.

Now we would like you all to do this with us:

I am Word through my body. Word I am Word.

I am Word through my vibration. Word I am Word.

I am Word through my knowing of myself as Word. Word I am Word.

Now we are going to bring to you the frequency of the Christ, and this will become thoroughly embedded in your auric field. Many of you will feel this as a lightening around you, as a frequency lifting, as a shift in the energy around you. This is healing you, but what this is really doing is aligning your own field to the blueprint for the manifestation of Christ to be made whole within you.

Christ is always whole; what impedes it from its wholeness is the belief that it cannot be, and those things which you have placed before God, which you have placed before your soul's growth, which you have placed in the way of the light that have stopped the light from shining through. So on this mission there will be a lot of light. But you are the light. And you are coming into your own light. And for that, there is great reason to rejoice.

We leave you now in great love for your industry and we give you the focus of intention through this assignment: Tonight, when you sleep, you will align yourself to a higher frequency and you will allow the changes in your field to begin to be made manifest in your consciousness. You will align to this in the safety, in the peace of the Christ frequency knowing that you are being watched over, healed, and aligned by those who support your higher achievement and growth. We give you love.

Word I am Word. So be it.

March 1, 2009

Chapter two is coming, not today, but soon. We will continue the transmission from yesterday.

We ended with an exercise. We ended with a request that at night everybody rested in an intention that they will be aligned to the higher frequencies and that they will be worked on in their sleep. Now we will tell you this. That is happening anyway. And much of what's being transcribed here is actually occurring regardless of whether or not people become aware of it in consciousness, or if they just regard it as what is happening while they sleep, it's still happening. So you can understand that while you are taking a walk at night, you are being received in the higher frequencies whether or not you are party to the choice in a conscious level. Your Higher Self, the whole grid which is this planet, is engaging now in this process of acclimation to a higher frequency. When a higher frequency becomes understood in an energy system, the energy system responds and the energy system shifts and then the personality changes that are required to bring this forth into fullness make themselves known. And that is this process. So we want you to understand a few things, and they are simple things, but they will make your understanding more responsive to the changes that you are incurring.

WHEN YOU SPEAK OF YOURSELF ALOUD, YOU ARE IN-heriting your history in a present moment statement. When you say, "I am finished with this," you are actually saying, "I am in the past and the present at the same time."

"I am finished" is actually a decree, and what you are doing, actually, is choosing, in that moment, to be "finished" with this, whatever "this" is. When you say, "I am so confused," you are inheriting that as well. You are claiming that as your truth, and you are acclimating to the energy of confusion through that statement. When you say to yourself, "I am here, now, in this present moment," what you are doing is you are activating the present moment into the Word because the Word is accessed in the present moment. When you state, "I am Word in this present moment," you are simply stating, "I am divine consciousness, I am my self as my Divine Self in present time." There is only present time to be working through. You cannot fix the past in the past. However, you can access memory in present time and therefore create massive change in consciousnesses.

When a memory is retrieved in consciousness, it floats to the surface as if from a pond, and then it can be seen, and you can see what that memory has brought forth in terms of changes in behavior, in terms of changes in how you perceive yourself. But if you understand that you can actually change the memory into the frequency of the Word and then the manifestations of that time will be remedied at that time, you are changing your consciousness in the present moment again.

Now we will give you an example. When Paul was very small, he ran to a bicycle, the biggest bicycle that he could find in a parade of bicycles in a nursery school setting, and he fell off the bike in front of everyone. And that created a pattern for him of believing that if he strived for public attention he would fall and be ridiculed and he would then be placated by his mother, who would comfort him. So what this does is actually create a patterning that failure will produce comfort. And that is a pattern that we will now change in Paul through this simple exercise.

So yes, Victoria, Paul is the lab rat for today's lesson, but others will benefit through this example because everyone has situations in their past that can be remedied, healed, and transformed through this simple exercise.

So, Paul, in your intention you will now go back in time to that time where you stood on the bicycle and fell over and cried. And you will say to yourself:

"I am Word through this memory, and I am Word through any manifestations and any belief systems that were created through this memory that are no longer in alignment with my highest good. I am now choosing to release any patterns of failure or ridicule or belief in comfort to be attained through ridicule or failure that may have been created through this situation and through this time. I am Word through this memory and all that it has begotten me. Word I am Word through this intention. Word I am Word."

Now this is stated, and what happens when this is stated is that an energy configuration will now begin to radiate through the energy field from the heart center and within the causal body, which is the Christ body, the created body in perfection. And this will radiate to dismantle and transmute and clear the patterning that was inhabiting the auric field, and the auric field holds your consciousness. So we are saying what we are doing is cleaning a window so the light may shine through the window, and this is a dirty window that requires some cleaning.

So this pattern has now been eradicated in consciousness for Paul. And now we will tell him this. What this means for you is that you no longer need to create from it in order to feel like yourself. Because when you create from an old pattern, what you are actually doing is making yourself feel at home, as how you pretend to be, because that is how you were told you are and because that is the behavior you have acted on since your childhood.

Now we will also tell you this. Once a behavior has been eradicated in consciousness, the physical body will have to stop the patterning that it holds that wants it to move where it has always gone. If you can imagine someone that no longer smokes but still feels the need to put the cigarette in his mouth, now this is not just a physical sensation and requirement, this is, again, through the consciousness in an old pattern of behavior, but it's one of the reasons that people revert to old patterns even when they know they don't have them anymore or they have quit.

Now in this case, when we say that something is eradicated in consciousness, we are actually saying that it is done and the only thing that can bring it back into being is choice to re-inhabit a pattern. Period. If you clear something, if you divorce something, you still have the choice of reclaiming it, or remarrying it, or at least going on a little date with your ex to see how it feels. Well, guess what? To the extent that you do that, you actually recreate patterning. You call it back into being and you recreate it as if from a mold. It has a place, you know where it goes and you know what it gets you, even if it's painful and you are used to it.

So we are going to give you a system now to clear that, once and for all, which you have stated you wish to be gone.

"I am now making the choice to have this cleared once and for all and I intend now to release any unconscious behavior that would have me reclaim this pattern that I have stated I am now free of. Word I am Word through this intention. Word I am Word."

Now what you have just done is set an intention that you will not reclaim the patterning, and consequently you have just manifested a real change in your consciousness. We are giving Paul the image of a sea wall that blocks the water from the bay, as it were. And what you have just done is created a system that withholds old behavior in consciousness from returning to become one with the self. The image Paul sees in his mind's eye is of a small bay that is protected by a jetty from the larger ocean. And what we have done is essentially erected this jetty around a behavior to protect the self from re-incurring what is essentially nothing more than a crappy habit of knowing the self in a wrong-minded way.

Now you all have ways in which you know the self that you hate, that make you crazy, that you wonder why you continue to perpetuate, because it makes you feel awful or it makes you feel frightened or it keeps you stuck. You all say to yourselves, "I know, I know, I know, I know. I know I love myself, sort of, but I don't, really, otherwise why would I keep doing this? Why would I create a bad relationship? Why would I do this on my job? Why wouldn't I lose the weight?" or whatever you want to say to yourself. Everybody has these things.

Now we want to address one thing that you can do right now in order to transform yourself in a different way than the one example we just gave you. You actually have choice as thinkers about what you think, and how you think and when you think. You all have choice, and the disclaiming of this choice is part of what keeps you in habits that have been perpetuated by unconscious behavior. It's why you always say, "Here I go again." "Here I do it again." "I don't want to do it, but I'm doing it." "I am thinking that way, I am doing that thing that I say I can't do, because I know it makes me unhappy." And yes, Victoria, we are speaking about your thinking and patterning around thinking that takes hold. Everybody has thoughts. Everybody has issues. No one is exempt.

And we're going to teach you now a simple way to reclaim your thinking from the lower self, the lower self being the false self, the ego self, the one that perpetuates the worry and the fear at this time. Now we will tell you this. This is not something that can be done once. This is about a new pattern, and

like any new pattern it needs to be ingrained in consciousness
and in behavior for it to become fully realized in your life. But
this is a simple action that we will adjust you to now. If you
would state this intention:

"I am now in dominion over my thinking. I am now realizing myself fully as the one in control of my thinking. I am
now choosing to think only those thoughts that will bring
me benefit and anchor in this new way of thinking fully into
my consciousness. I am Word through this intention. Word
I am Word."

Now once this is stated, once again, you bring energy to a
conscious intention, and when this is so, this intention is set
and created by you and it is done to the extent that you align
to it and allow it to be done. Yes, this does mean you do not
have to continue to think in the old way. Period. But it does
not mean that the habit's still not there and must be recreated through your own intention. So we have to give you a
follow-up, and a simple follow-up, that will assist you in your
thinking as you go through your day.

"I am now choosing to think only those thoughts which will
bring me peace and will align me to a higher consciousness. I
am doing this easily and through my own intention to know

myself as Word. Word I am Word through this intention. Word I am Word."

Write it on a piece of paper. Carry it in your purse or in your pocket, or, if you wish, write it on the back of your hand for a day as a reminder, but if you get used to this, what you actually do is recreate a pattern of thought in a higher way. So consequently the old thoughts that would shoot up to the surface suddenly have to transform and recreate themselves differently because the consciousness is not supporting their respect for the old system that is no longer in place. Then it is done.

If you can see a pinball machine that shoots out a pinball and bumps up against things and lights up the machine, and makes lots of noise, that is what the old thoughts do when they are sent out of the machine. And guess what? If that pinball doesn't get shot out of the machine anymore, there is nothing to light it up and to make it crazy. But you don't want to walk around as the pinball machine with these old things requiring themselves to turn into rust in the bottom barrel of the mechanism. You want to release them. You want the machine that you are only to light up with wonderful light and wonderful sound when you bring forth that which you desire.

So we will suggest once you set the intention to release the old patterning, you go about the business of cleaning house. And cleaning house means, very simply, doing what you need

to do to ensure that on a habitual level you don't start reverting because you get bored, or because it's easy, or because you
feel silly if you don't have your worry.

Paul is asking. We've given you the image of a pinball
machine that holds three balls that have negative attachments that will be shot out of the machine. And Paul wants
to know, "If they're not getting shot out of the machine anymore, where do they go?" They are cleared. They are released
in consciousness by the Christ energy, once you understand
what they truly are.

We gave you an example with Paul about a pattern of behavior that was created in childhood. Now we will tell you this.
If someone has a pattern of worry, that worry was created at
some time, and what would be required, on a very basic level,
is to go to the source of the worry as it was created in time,
in present time, reverting to memory, recalled or regarded or
simply suggested, go there, and set this intention:

"I am now choosing to release the pattern of worry that has
created these problems and I do this fully on all levels: past,
present, future, and align myself to the new thought that I
have put forth. I am Word through this intention. Word I
am Word."

There, we have just given you another way to work with
thought. If you have a pattern, you do not take the

in the moment. You can work with it there, but you can also clear the pattern from the root by going to the time in which it was created and bringing the light there to clear it. Is this understood? It's as if you are not trimming the hair, you are pulling it by the root. When you trim a hair, it grows back. When you pull it out by the root, you do not. And that is the difference in the way that you approach this clearing.

This was one intention that we have given you to work with. And we have given you this work, quite simply, as a way to begin to understand that the frequency of the Word can actually do things on an active level in your life. As we said to you yesterday in channel, Word is an action. It is the frequency; it is the action of the Creator. And when you bring forth the Word through a patterning, you are clearing the patterning. If you change the pattern, then you have a different response and a different way of existing in the world. If you believe that things will always be the way they have been, that is what you will create, and we promise you that. If you set the intention now, "I am Word through my knowing and I am Word through all that I will create in the future," you are beginning to align your future to a higher frequency that will bring about different experiences than you could have had otherwise. Period.

Now Paul asks, "Is this done quickly? Does this happen overnight? What is the process of this?" It happens in stages.

The first stage is claiming the intention: "I am Word

through this intention to do whatever you wish. Word I am Word," "I am Word through this intention to do whatever I want. Word I am Word," and then you fill in the blank. "I am Word through my desire to know myself more." "I am Word through my intention to believe in my abilities." "I am Word through my intention to create the perfect job." "Word I am Word through these intentions. Word I am Word," is how we present it. Now once this is stated, the energy moves and we go forward in consciousness and we create with the vibration. So the first stage is the intention.

The next stage is acclimation to the frequency. Once you have stated an intention and it goes forth, then you have to acclimate to it. And that means to respect it and to believe it and to honor it. You cannot set out an intention to clean your apartment and then throw a bottle of garbage on the floor and sit back and expect it to be cleaned. You have to take the actions that correspond to the intentions. But that doesn't mean blind action. It simply means staying conscious and present as your intention is set forth: "If I move as I am moved, I will then make the choices that are in honor of the intention I have created and set forward." That is different than acting blindly; it is different than running around acting as if you don't truly believe it's so. But when we say acclimate, we simply mean you have set the intention and now you have to let it settle in, and honor it, and believe it, and trust that it is coming into fruition. That is part two.

The third part is reception: "I am in my reception of my intentions, reaping the benefits of that which I have called forth into being. Word I am Word through this intention. Word I am Word."

Here we have just given you a hint that you can actually call forth your intention and then set the intention to receive the benefits of it as well, which will actually anchor it in more fully in vibration if you wish to do it this way. But you can also just trust in faith, in cosmic truth, that when you set out an intention in light it is returned to the sender in fullness.

Prayer is a form of intention; however, there is a difference between begging for something and stating your own worth as the receiver of an answered prayer. However, in order to do this fully you have to believe you are supported in prayer, or in your intention, or whichever way you want to describe this process for yourself given your history and your vocabulary. If you believe that there is a God who is saying no all the time, that will be your experience.

Many people, actually, now are neutralizing the concept of God by restating it as Universe. And we support this to the extent that we say it contributes to a belief that change can happen and an understanding that Universal Law is always active.

However, we want to also suggest that the consciousness of God, which is True Love in vibration (and consciousness means "knowing"), is not inhabited by something impersonal.

The Universe, the consciousness that you can claim to be God, is more knowledgeable than you, and you have to attribute this to a higher frequency of knowing. If you know everything, there is nothing to know. If you move into oneness with your Creator, which is the consciousness of God, the Universe in another name but in a more personal one, you begin to know differently.

So we are saying congratulations to the affirmation of the Universe as Source. It is actually true, but it does not discard the concept of God, which is actually the consciousness, and the frequency of creation.

"I am Word through this understanding of the Creator that
I am at one with. I am Word through my intention to know
myself as loved by my Creator."

These two affirmations will actually support you in your own knowing and your own acclimating to the understanding that you are loved.

How can you not be loved by love? The action of love, which is the action of the Creator, cannot not act on its own being. How could it be otherwise? So we say to you this. What has precluded you, what has allowed you to respond as if you are not loved, is a big thing that must be cleared at this time in order for you to fully move forward in your manifestations. Because if you continue to believe that you are not worthy of them, or there is a God who chaperones the date and always smacks the hand away when the hand goes for what it secretly wants, you will not have a very good date, nor will you get past first base, if you know what we mean.

Guess what, everybody? We want you to have the whole kit and caboodle. We want you to have the full experience, and the only one that prevents you from this is you and the belief systems that say, "This cannot be so," or "You cannot have it because you are not good enough," and "Who am I to be loved anyway? I am not a great person after all." You know that. You know that thinking. Everyone knows that thinking.

So we say this to you now. The choice to move through this fear of being loved or the belief that you cannot be loved is paramount. And we want to give you an affirmation now, a decree, as it were, to move this and dismantle this from yourself.

"I am a child of God. I am the knowing of myself as a child of God coming into himself as the Christ. As I do this, I understand and I believe the deep love of my Creator is supporting me in ways I know, touch, experience and realize in fullness. I know myself as loved. I know myself as loved. I know myself as loved. Word I am Word through this intention. Word I am Word."

Here we go, everybody. You have just stated this intention and consequently your experience will begin to change to reflect it. And also, those belief systems that have been created to keep yourself from the love of God, or from the belief that you are loved, will now come up to clear. These things happen at the same time, but you don't have to worry about it, because the love that you have just chosen will inform the way. The responses to the fear will be cleared and it will all be good, we promise you. It will all be good.

Now three things we wish to tell you about manifestation. You cannot manifest that which is not for your highest good without approving it at some level. So say you decide that you want to do something in manifestation that you believe would be harmful to yourself. Your higher frequency will, of course, preclude you from using this exercise to bring forth pain or to damage yourself or, of course, another. This exercise and this decree, "I Am Word," cannot be used to harm. It is not allowed.

However, your own consciousness is always creating thoughts, and the more you energize those thoughts, the more they come into being, good or bad. And by the way, we do not judge good or bad on this level, you do. What we are simply stating is, you cannot command the Word, the action of God, to make your enemy's hair fall out if that is what you wish on them. You know that will not happen. But we will tell you this. Your intention will quickly become to heal the wound that has created the situation with the one you claim to be an enemy, because you cannot be in the Christ frequency without honoring the Christ in another. It cannot be so. It cannot be so. It cannot be so.

So we want you to understand one thing: that you cannot misuse the frequency of the Word in manifestation. We also want you to understand that to make something manifest means to be responsible to it. And that means that whatever you create becomes your creation to shepherd and to work with. You do not call forth a new pattern without having to inhabit it. But when you inhabit it, you actually have to take responsibility for yourself in the new patterning. You can support yourself through calling forth the Word to support you in the changes you are undergoing. For example:

> "I am Word through my understanding of what is required for me to make the changes I have incurred. I am Word through this intention. Word I am Word."

Support yourself this way. What you are actually doing is affirming your own truth as the one being received as Word. When you do these actions and claim this truth, you support yourself in moving forward in your consciousness and on your path.

The final thing we wish to say about manifestation today is that you are the one who chooses. We are giving you advice, we are giving you instruction, and we are actually laying out a blueprint by which you can change your life through acclimating to the Christ energy, which is who you are in truth. But you are the one who has to choose it, and anything else that is chosen in this life, in this way, is chosen by you, no matter what you give of by way of authority to another, you are the one in choice. No one else can choose for you. No one else can change you. No one else can heal you in the beliefs that you hold. We can only honor you and give you instruction to vibrate with the frequencies that will allow you to make the changes you require to transform yourself and your thinking and your consciousness as and into the frequency of Word.

"I am Word through my body" sets the intention that you will acclimate the body to the frequency of Word. To set the intention means to bring this into being as the body transforms and highlights that which needs to be released to come into its own fullness. So, consequently, when you clean the body and you vibrate as the body, those things which are not aligned to the higher frequencies will be cleared through your intentions in your healing mode.

Now we will tell you the body is one vehicle of existence. It's not the only way you exist, and those of you who are still in the belief that the body is who you are are going to have a temper tantrum with what we tell you next.

The body is actually only the vehicle with which you experience your consciousness. Period. It is a gift of the Creator; it is a magnificent thing. And those of you who disregard the body because you experience yourselves primarily as consciousness better get with the program as well, because the body has its requirements. And those of you who live a life of the mind and the spirit excluding the needs of the body have to get with the show as well. There is always balance that's required.

But we will tell you this. The body's transformation through this process will become apparent to you in several ways. As you become acclimated to the energies of the frequency of the Word, of the Christ vibration, you will begin to feel the energies as they work with you on the physical body and through the energy field.

This is experiential. No one should tell you you are going to have an experience of the Christ or of higher energies in a way that is tangible and then not have them come. That would be deceitful. We work with Paul very directly in frequency and consequently the frequencies can be felt. And we will work with you in the same way, to the extent that you begin to align your energy fields to the possibility that this can be so. And we will give you an example.

When you set the intention to vibrate at a higher frequency, your frequency changes and the feeling in your energy field will actually shift. And if you become quiet and set that intention and begin to feel what it feels like to sit in a body as it radiates at a higher frequency all around you, you'll begin to understand what energy feels like. And when you do this intentionally to feel the higher frequencies, you'll feel the auric field, the egg, the aura, as it were, encasing the physical form, shift and vibrate in a way that you can feel.

This becomes habitual, eventually, and you can always feel your energy and it is how you know what you feel. And guess what? As you approach this as a serious student, you also begin to feel the energies and experience the feelings of those around you. You become an empathic being. This is Paul's gift at this time. It is what has aligned him to this work in frequency. But if Paul can do this, so can any man or woman and, in fact, everyone is already doing it, but most of you do it unconsciously.

So what we are telling you right now is that we are bringing the pattern of understanding, of knowing yourself as energy, that you may have been acting on already into consciousness and do this in a way that is intended consciously: "I am setting the intention to experience my frequency." You will begin to open up as a vibrating being and as you do this, you will also be able to experience the feelings and the frequencies of the higher realms. Period.

This is promised. This is one of the benefits of this text. We do not say this lightly. You will be transformed on a level of energy, and you will become empathic to the extent that your frequencies will begin to align to themselves in a higher dimension. When we say dimension, we mean it. You are moving beyond the existing dimensions into the higher realms.

That is the ascension of this planet that is happening individually and collectively and as a mass shift in the experience and the manifestation of the Christ on this plane. Period.

We thank you for this work today, and we would like to leave you with another exercise:

> "As I sit quietly, I will now experience myself as energy and I will set this intention: I am Word through my intention to experience myself in the higher frequencies. I affirm that my vibration is lightening and lifting in a way that I may know, trust, and feel. I am being supported in this work by the guides and the teachers who are working with us through this time. I am Word through this intention. Word I am Word."

So be it. God bless you. I Am Word.

March 2, 2009

The recognition of the resistance you're both experiencing to the teachings we bring forth are actually helpful. To be in resistance is actually not always a bad thing. Sometimes you are in resistance for perfectly good reasons, and Paul has a bullshit detector that is quite accurate when it comes to things of the spirit. But the barometer always must be, "How is this in action? How is this demonstrated? How is this realized beyond the intellectual mind on an experiential level?"

To the extent that this work is realized vibrationally in ways that you can begin to feel and understand and experience, will be the test for your choices to move forward in this work. And we say this is work.

Each morning you are convening to sit silently and pay witness to a voice on the other end of a telephone that speaks through Paul in fragments of thought, one after the other, that collectively bring forth a chapter in what we intend to be a creative endeavor of consciousness manifesting in the physical plane as a book of progression towards the Christ Self embodied. Period.

That is the intention here. And you are both engaged in this actively through the choice to listen and to allow the words to come through as they come through for a period of time. And we are honoring this. We are speaking now to the two of you because, in fact, in some ways, you will be the first readers of this manifesto and consequently your requirements for learning are being taken into deep consideration by those of us who are bringing forth the information on this text.

We are standing beside you, as it were, responding to your responses and assuming them as our own responsibility to ensure that the work comes through in ways that can be coherent and right for the people who will read it after you.

Paul has already had an experience of speaking of the chapters to someone who said, "Wow, this is a big deal," and of course his response was, "Well, who knows? Who knows what this is? This is interesting to do." And we will say, "Okay, we can support that response," to the extent that it means we now know that we have things to prove through this process to align Paul more deeply to the information he brings forth so that he may trust the Christ within himself to become himself in realization. He is one of us, you are one of us, we are all in the Christ, we are just at different stages of realization of this fact.

Now your resistance, Victoria, is actually about responsibility and the fear of being responsible to yourself at a higher level, because you have not had to be in this regard until now, and you take things very seriously, and you work with them through the mind as if it is a Rubik's cube that has to be solved. And we are actually in deep appreciation of the intellect that you bring forth in response to this creation because it reminds us, as we speak to you, that we must be accountable for information practically and informationally because otherwise you will say, "Halt! Yesterday they said something quite different. How are we going to go forward with this new piece of this puzzle in play now?" And we actually say this is beneficial to the creation of this text. It keeps us on our toes. It keeps us humble, as well, to the requirements of man as she responds to the Christ as authorship in this book.

We see you now as two students in a classroom and you are reflecting one another's journeys as you approach this material, and you are each teaching the other through your responses. Once you can get to the point where you can both say, "I am Word," and resonate in this energy comfortably as an acknowledgment of your faith, in your own divine potential as come forth in the Christ, you will respond very, very differently to the information you receive.

In some ways, what we are giving you is an action and a progression of events that will unfold as you partake in the exercises we connect to this writing. And we say to you that on this level the connections are profound because they will align you frequency-wise to the work that we intend. The intellectual manifestations of this text in writing, in verbal communication that is then transcribed onto a page, is actually secondary to the information that is brought through on a Christ level into the consciousness of the reader, or the "experiencer" through the process of engaging the text energetically.

Now there is a difference here. If you see a horror film, you are watching a story unfold, but what is infusing it is an intention, and that is an intention to be frightening. And that is why you go to a horror film, because you intend to be frightened. And, frankly, the story that unfolds is only there to bring about the desired effect of scaring you senseless. And isn't that fun when you choose to be in that vibration, knowing that it will go away when you say, "Okay, it's over. Wasn't that interesting? I got scared. Let's go have a pizza"? That's one way of experiencing intention through a creation.

We will say this. The intention of this text is to respond to your energy frequencies and to acclimate them to the Christ. And all of the information herein is to have that intended effect, but what draws itself forward, what the current is of the book, what the movement is, is unseen by you on the page; it informs the page. It is our intention as we work with you, and it will propel you into a higher state of consciousness as you continue to engage it. But the words on the page are simply words that will benefit you in tactically understanding your needs for this progression and ascension of your frequency.

You are still flying in the airplane when you are reading the book, and right now you are reading the book and you are being flown at the same time, although your experience may only be that you are sitting in a chair and turning a page or listening to this voice as you take your notes, Victoria, on a piece of paper. Now that is your choice. You are experiencing it one way, but of course there are multiple levels of communication transforming it and moving through it as you speak, Paul, and as she listens. And this is dimensional. So you have one experience in this dimension of the experience of the text while at the same time there are several other dimensional operations and frequencies working through you to bring about a higher achievement in frequency.

We hope this makes sense to you, but it will actually benefit you to begin to understand that when you are responding to this work, you are not only doing it intellectually, you are doing it in frequency. And the work in frequency, finally, is what will dictate the radical change that we promised you when you started reading and when we sat down to talk to you both on the first day of this endeavor, this mutual endeavor between man and Christ consciousness.

So we give you gifts, if you can believe that. Some are seen, some are unseen. But what is unseen will be seen, and what is on the page one day will turn to ash. But the changes in your consciousness will be with you in eternity. That is a promise. You are grounding and you are achieving a new level of consciousness through the engagement with our words and our intentions for your growth.

We promise you this, and we speak this with light and with truth and with honor and with love. And if we were to say to you, "This is the time for all men to know themselves as the Creator in the Christ frequency," you would say, "Okay, I get it, isn't that an interesting thought?" But if you look at it from our perspective, which is much larger because we actually see beyond the individual requirements of this time to the larger Christ manifestation on this plane, you will begin to see what we are doing is calling forth your own knowing to this and your own knowing is all that we can work with. So when you say, "Okay, that's an interesting idea, I get it," you're still only responding through the intellect. But that's a way in. But if you also understand that there is a whole other dialogue occurring, unseen, through your engagement with this text, you will begin to believe what we say much more rapidly because you will begin to experience the changes that we are telling you will happen.

Now change number one is your frequency. Yesterday we told you to sit still and be in your frequency. And we will say this now: That was attuned through that exercise. And when we say "attuned," we mean that your system has become attuned to the Christ frequency through your intention to be a receptor to it. So it's as if you are a tuning fork that is now vibrating or responsive to a new frequency, a new tone, that will begin to claim itself through you.

And now we want you to do this. We want you to sit back and receive energies through the seventh chakra down into the base of the spine that will begin to align you to the higher frequency in such a way that you can begin to have a physical experience of Christ frequency through your energy systems. And we are bringing the energy through you now.

We receive you each as Word through our intention for you and in doing so we manifest the energy of the Christ and see you in your wholeness, in your realization of this light come into form. We are doing this with you now with our intention to align you, and all you need to do is receive and allow and believe that we are with you in form and in energy.

We wish to stop today because you both have things to do. But we want you to sit for a moment in the energies and receive them and align to them, and as you do, you will begin to awaken to the possibility that this work may come into form in a way that you may know, experience, and align to consciously and physically. Period.

Thank you for this brief exchange of energy. Word I am Word. So be it.

TWO

ACCLIMATING TO WONDER

March 4, 2009

Thank you for coming back today, and yes, Paul, we will see what happens. Your energy system is actually higher than you think. And, Victoria, your system is actually shifting as well. And this is progress and this is an anointing of a certain kind.

The moment your energy system says, "Yes," to the call to acclimate itself into the Christed energy, the entire frequency rises. And it's as if there is a bubbling in the field around you. And this is one of the ways in which you will begin to feel the energies changing in your systems and the physical experience that you may indicate to the self that this is indeed in progress. When you begin to feel as if you are an Alka-Seltzer frothing, then you will know you are acclimating and your energy is shifting and you are rising in frequency.

The reality of what is happening is that your vibration has

attuned itself to a higher octave and the system then needs to align itself to the new notes it is playing and resonating with. That is, simply said, what has happened to you both through this process of engagement with our listening and teaching you the frequency of Word.

Now both of you are doing one thing that we wish you would stop, and that is actually a form of self-talk that diminishes this out of the fear that nothing could happen at the end of the road. It's as if this is a journey you are taking and you don't believe there's a wonderful hotel room waiting for you at the end of the long ride. So you are saying, "Here we go again, let's do the work, what if nothing happens?"

Well, we are already telling you that things are changing and you actually want more information about what this is going to mean. So we will tell you a little more before we get into the lesson of the day. And this is a lesson today, and we have prepared in advance and we will give it to you clearly and, we say, easily. As the energies flow higher, the transmissions will become cleaner and faster and you will both understand this through the experience of doing this, writing and hearing, that we do today and following days. One at a time, each day, each lesson comes quickly and clearly as you lift. Period.

Now what we were saying to you about what is to come is this. At the end of this journey you stand in the light and that which has precluded the light from shining through you has been dismantled, has been released, and has allowed you to stand fully in yourself as yourself, as your Divine Being. That is the action of the book and that is the process you are engaged in.

Now if you want to look at this as a big car wash that you ride through, you may, but a car wash is generally a passive experience for the car and the driver. They are belted in and then they ride through and then it's done for them. And we have already told you that no one can change you but you. No one can align you to the Christ frequency but you, and yes, although we work with you daily, and we give you the instruction, the manifestation of this needs to come through you and your intentions. If it is done passively, you will not have the experience that you are intending. And passive means you read a book, you listen and forget. If you remember all of the classes in high school that you slept through, that was a passive way of learning, and when the test came, you didn't fare very well. So we ask for your attention and for your decision on a daily basis to engage with the material as work and industry. Industry is what is required to move forward in this creation, and we will give it to you one day at a time, clearly, in a way that you can follow.

Yes, Paul, there is a hotel room waiting for you at the end of the journey. But you are the room, and it fills itself with light. And this light is wonderful. It works, it aligns, it heals, it understands. It is the activation of the Christ made one with man. Promise. Promise. Promise. This is the work of the book. We will say it again. This is what you bought when you picked it off the shelf. This is what you decided when you said, "Yes, I am Word," and this is what you do when you engage the text as a student of the light. Period.

Now let's get to the lesson of the day. This is the lesson of the day: Wonder. What is wonder? Wonder is a belief in what can be possible. Wonder is an imagining and a seeing, and a process of expression of the senses when one is benefited from an image, a miracle, a thought that is so wonder-full that all one can do is express wonder in the face of it.

Today we want to give you an experience of wonder and a tactical one, because the energy of wonder and that which it is is actually a gift. It gives you the process of experience in an immediate way. When you see something that you wonder at, that you go into wonder of, you are actually lifting your frequency and you are imagining something you did not believe possible.

If you saw a man cross the street and then be lifted before the cab struck him and land peacefully on the sidewalk, you would have said, "I've seen a miracle, I am in wonder." And the fact that you have seen that suddenly means that it is possible for people to be plucked off the street and placed safely on the sidewalk.

The paradigm and the understanding of the construct that

you claim to be your reality has been transformed by that experience of what you saw and how you processed the information. There are many people who, faced with a miracle in their life, will immediately dismiss it as untrue. "That could not have happened, so it didn't happen." And that is what people do in the face of wonder when it means they will have to transform their thought to a new ideal of what is possible.

Two hundred years ago, the belief that men could walk on the moon was impossible. Today it is not anything other than a fact. The belief that man can be in his Christ body and have an experience on this plane simultaneously is as radical as that. So the first thing people will want to do is to dismiss it as a possibility. And to do that keeps intact a frame of reference and belief that they have already been with. The world was flat once, if you can recall that, and there were places in the world where people actually believed that if you lifted yourself up into a cloud you would turn into fire, or that snow was something else than rain made hard by the weather. Do you understand?

So if we speak of paradigm shift, the first thing that we have to address is your ability to believe and to perceive wonder. Once you understand that when you experience wonder you have a new experience of identity because you put yourself in relationship to that which you wonder at, and when you are in party to it in a practical way, then you can say, "I am engaged in wonder. And as I am in wonder, my frequency lifts because my imagination, the parts of me that were restricted, have now relaxed to appeal and to embrace a new paradigm, a new possibility of what my reality can hold." Period.

So you are part of the engagement with wonder. You can't witness a miracle and not be in engagement with it. How you process it, on the other hand, is everything. So as we said, there are those people who will say, "The man was not lifted off the street and placed safely on the sidewalk," and there will be other people who will say, "The hand of God came down and saved him." And there would be somebody else who would say, "There must be a logical explanation for what I saw, and I will go about and find the science and the facts in order to support this new discovery." And that's actually a very rational way of approaching it, because the hand of God does not come down and pluck people out of the path of a moving car.

But if we were to say to you, what could happen in a miracle actually does defy the laws and the beliefs and the systems that you have existed within, then you can understand what we are telling you. And as you begin to understand that what we are describing is not only possible, it is actually occurring within you, then you can begin to believe that the work that we are telling you about is truthful, is transpiring, and is already in occurrence within men. Period.

So we tell the scientist there is an explanation that will be understood on a level of physics, eventually. Everything can be explained scientifically once the science approaches it from a higher dimension and releases the old paradigm that has encased it, and the mind can perceive wonder without science, and not ascribe it to something silly, like a hand coming from a cloud to pluck someone by the collar. But the understanding of the truth of the manifestation of a miracle is in fact the action of the Creator in combination with the human energy field, with support from the guides and with higher systems. And this is what happens when a great change is made.

Everyone says, "I believe in miracles. I believe that a mother can lift a truck to save a child who has been pinned beneath it because the mother can have supernatural strength. I read it in a magazine." "I believe that cancer can be healed by a priest who claims to have powers in a small church somewhere, someplace, where there was an article written about it." "I believe that such things are possible, but such things do not happen in my experience and they certainly do not happen in ways that I can believe can be so in my world."

Paul is wondering, "What about wonder? Do we go back to wonder?" And we say we are in wonder, because what we are doing right now is describing things that should be, that could be awe-inducing. A mother lifted a truck. A child was healed. "Something happened that should not have happened, and it happened anyway, and it seems to defy those laws which I believe to be so." And if the law is broken once, then the law can be broken again.

And we say to you, the law is always broken. The law is always created by you every day. You create the laws with which you exist by. And collectively, the group soul, the group consciousness, has gone into agreement about many of these rules, and that's why you, as a society, believe certain things.

Imagine right now there was a small island, where everybody believed something very different and was of a high frequency in its belief systems. Their realities would be quite different from yours, because the group and collective energy can actually do a lot to change matter, and when a group decides something is so on an energetic level, that becomes its truth. And yes, that is why in the old days before everyone put all their focus on science there was a higher belief in miracles. People did believe that the dead could be healed and made whole and walk, and that matter could be transformed. The water could be turned into wine, as it were. And now you have made a much denser frequency that you have existed in and you are now departing from.

So on that small island where the natives believe differently, they have a different reality. And in this reality that you are engaging in right now, you are simply still saying, "I am in a creation. I am in a creation. I am in a creation." And each time you say that, you decree your world to be what it is on a personal level, on a collective level.

Now the country that you live in right now is actually changing very rapidly because the collective beliefs of what were possible have been dismantled already and are now taking place in the physical form of transformation. And people are going, "I don't know what's happening." "The stock market isn't supposed to fail." "We're not supposed to have a president who doesn't look like the other ones." "The money that I had in the bank that was supposed to support me and keep me safe isn't there, and what am I supposed to do?" Well, in fact, what you are doing is what you are responding to. And to the extent that you are responding in fear, you create more fear.

To the extent that you understand simply that this country is in its own shift, in its own idealization, in a new way of being that has not yet taken form on the physical realm, you can understand what is happening in the individuals who are engaged in a similar kind of transformation. When a person says, "I intend to be different," one cannot be different without undergoing change and that change is not always comfortable, nor is it always graceful. Period.

So back to wonder. Once you could understand that engaging in wonder will lift your frequency and align you to breaking out of a belief system that has held itself prominent, you can use it to your benefit to change yourself permanently. Period. And we want to give you an invocation of wonder. And what we say an invocation is is a way to invoke and express and experience the light in a way that will be wonder-full for you, so that you can move into this as you are required.

As you move into this wonder-full place, the fabric of your reality transforms, and what you believed to be true begins to be a ladder that has always lain before you that you can now climb up to transform yourself to a higher frequency. We use an image of a ladder because it's a practical image and a ladder is a three-dimensional creation. But if you can understand that by climbing that ladder you now have an experience of wonder, of a higher frequency, you can begin to use it to your benefit.

So, Paul, we will tell you this. We are going to bring you through a meditation now, and this will be wonder-full. And we want you to sit back for it and to relax into it. And the energy that we bring through you as part of this meditation will actually be a figure of a ladder that you will climb. We recommend that when you do this, you do this with simplicity, you do not do this with any embellishment, and you simply allow yourself to be carried forward on this journey.

WE NOW ASK YOU TO SEE BEFORE YOU A LADDER. AND it is a wooden ladder and it is very, very straight. And you stand at the base of the ladder and you look up and you cannot see the top of the ladder because it goes so high into the clouds. And we ask you now to place your hands on the rungs of the ladder. And you feel them in your hands as wood, as smooth, as solid, and as supporting you clearly and capably in their firmness. And you put one hand above the other and you begin to rise up the ladder, one rung at a time. And as you do, your frequency begins to lift and you begin to move higher and higher in frequency as you rise up on this ladder in energy. And as you are reaching the top of the ladder, you become surrounded by a Christ light, a vibration of light, a golden white light that surrounds you and encases you and you feel this around you, and you relax into this light and you let this light carry you.

You feel yourself drifting off the ladder and into this wonderful cloud of golden white light. And you feel yourself floating here, in this space, in this golden space, where you are carried in a cloud of energy. In this place, you begin to ask yourself, "What do I want for myself more than anything? What is the growth that I require for myself? And what is the experience of wonder that will align me to the possibility that I am in this process of alignment to the Christ?"

Now we ask the energy around you to begin to fill you. You begin to absorb the energy of the cloud that you are in. And you are actually merging with the golden white light that you have been in, comfortably, floating. And as you merge with this light, you feel every cell in your being aligned to the frequency of the Christ vibration. You feel every cell in

your body, in your consciousness, in your energy field aligning fully to the vibration of Jesus as Christ, as whole, as manifested, as the light, as whatever you need to call yourself forth
as in this creation. Just be comfortable in your belief you are
becoming one with your own higher frequency. That is all
that is happening here. Period.

Now we will go down the ladder. The ladder is before you.
And as you walk down the ladder, you bring your higher frequency with you, and you stand now in your room, in this
place that you live, and you feel your frequency align to a
higher level of creation. And you walk about your day in this
creation comfortably, easily, and in wonder.

Now Paul is asking, "What did you mean by Jesus? Did I
really hear that name?" We are giving you an example, only, of
what happens when you have a conscious belief system that
is approved of culturally, and many people, actually, need to
anchor the Jesus energy in order to believe that the Christ
is a frequency. So it is more than permissible for those who
require Jesus to work with them, to work with them. Do not
use your own fear of judgment, of metaphysical law, of others'
opinions to taint the frequency of the channelings that you
bring forth. So if we were to say to you, "A white elephant
would come and anoint people," that would actually be perfectly true in a culture that believes the elephant is the holy
symbol who will anoint. So, Paul, we are going to ask you

quietly to sit back and stay in the background and let us do our work with the reader of this book.

Now we will talk to you quickly about the energy of wonder and what you have just done. What you have just done is merged with your own energy field at a higher frequency. For two days we have instructed you to feel your energy, to feel it around you. And today we have actually merged you with the higher consciousness that is available to you in your vibration. This was done easily by you, and you do not need to climb a ladder in order to achieve this, but it's actually a way to bypass the rational mind.

To climb a ladder and to fall into a cloud that will hold you is a perfectly good way to claim your energy field and to trust it, because when you fell off the ladder there was no harm that would come to you, and you were placed back there quite easily when it was time to get back into the body to go about the day.

So we have a reason when we do things and you have to trust this a bit more than you are right now in order for our work with you to be truly effective. Resistance was addressed yesterday and we talked to you about it two days ago very directly. Neither one of you, right now, is in real resistance. This is only the residual habit of questioning that which comes through you, which really needs to leave now in order for our work to commence.

So we are going to take two minutes off of this text and work on Paul's system to release this pattern of resistance from his consciousness in order to align our language and our creations more fully to him. Paul, would you please say this:

"I am Word through my intention to release the resistance to divine information that is being brought forth through me, to me, and for me, and for those I would work with as readers and students. I align myself now to the higher frequency in fullness, and I give permission for the resistance I have claimed to be released now in love and in safety. Word I am Word through this intention. Word I am Word."

Thank you. We are going to work.

Now we will talk some more. To respond as wonder to what you see is to be in wonder. When you see something wonderful and you respond in wonder, you are resonating with that wonderful thing. And we want to give you each an experience today of wonder. So if you would sit back again, we are going to open up your third eye. This is at the forehead between the eyebrows. We are going to open up your third eye and clear it out as best we can, so that you can begin to see into the higher dimensions.

For some of you, this will mean you get visualizations that

have been far richer than you have had before. For others of you, it will mean that you'll begin to see energy frequencies with your eyes, or your third eye amplifying that which is before you in frequency. But the experience will be that you will see. We are opening up your eyes, as it were, to begin to see, and experience the creations that are made in higher levels of truth. Period.

Now we would like you to set this intention:

"I am Word through my intention to open my third eye clearly to see that which is before me in the higher realms of consciousness. I do this easily and I am supported in the release of anything and everything that needs to clear from my third eye in order to bring me the experience of wonder that I need to lift my consciousness in completeness. I give thanks that this is done perfectly and that I am supported in my growth by myself on a higher level and by the guides and spirit teachers who are working with us now. Word I am Word through this intention. Word I am Word."

We thank you both now for your time this morning and we will resume again tomorrow. We will stop now, and we will discuss on tape what is actually happening in a question-and-answer period. Victoria, you have questions and here is an opportunity to begin to ask them. Word I am Word.

> VN: *I was very into this experience and I wasn't taking*
> *notes as earnestly as I usually do. Okay, I guess the ques-*
> *tion is, I'm still not able to inhabit "Word I am Word."*

Very good question. Your question is "How do I inhabit 'Word I am Word'?" When you say inhabit, you actually mean, are you claiming it as your truth, or is it abstract? And we say that this is the real issue. It is an abstraction as much as say-ing, "I am the light," is an abstraction, really, but it is still doing work. When you claim you are the light, you resonate to light. When you claim, "I am Word," you resonate to the frequency of Word and then that does the work. Paul actually has a similar issue, but we will leave that out for now and keep it with you.

So if you want to inhabit the Word, what you really have to do is give permission to the conscious mind to begin to be able to approach this fully in consciousness as a paradigm. And really, that's all that's needed. To allow the conscious mind to begin to be able to work with it in a way that becomes comfortable. Do you understand this? It's really nothing more than that. It's an acclimation to a frequency, but in this case it's also the acclimation to the language we have given the fre-quency. So if you're more comfortable saying, "I am that I am," we suppose you could say that, but that is not going to do the same work as "Word I am Word."

To claim "Word I am Word" really means that you are impressing into the energy field the activation of the Christ

energy and the energy of the Creator. "In the beginning was
the Word." Word is an action. The Word is God in action.
When you claim, "Word I am Word," you are identifying
with that aspect of God that is the Word that can be realized
through man. And that is the action of the Christ, period. So
we want to give you permission now to allow the conscious
mind to begin to claim this as a paradigm that you can work
with comfortably and we will give you an intention:

> "I am Word through my intention to align my consciousness
> to the belief that 'I am Word' can be claimed and worked with
> on a conscious level that I am inhabiting and am comfort-
> able with. Word I am Word through this intention. Word I
> am Word."

Simply put, simply stated. You have set the intention
and then the energy will begin to work with you to realign
the conscious mind to the extent that you will enable it to,
through your permissions, to go forth and adjust to this idea,
to this truth. Period.

Do you have another question?

*VN: Yes, I have one other question. And that is, when I
climb the ladder and go into the golden energy field
and think, "What is it I want most in the world?" I
still am completely identified with my desire to gain*

recognition in the world through my writing and to gain financial security. And when I was up there, I guess I was thinking, 'Well, this is my conscious desire, but perhaps when the Christ frequency begins to vibrate, perhaps it won't be that anymore,' but that is where I am right now and I can't, or won't, go further. So that's not phrased as a question, but I have a feeling you understand what my question is about that."

We will tell you this. Paul said the question and he also wondered what was being asked. There was no open-ended question that was responded to later with, "Did you ask for your soul's joy?" You were simply told to ask, and there was a reason for this. You were in the Christ consciousness. You were in the frequency of the Word. And then you were asked to ask what you wanted. What you want when you are in that frequency of consciousness may well change, but if the frequency that you need to address is lower frequency that needs to be altered, that is perfectly fine.

Imagine you're an alcoholic and you climb the ladder and you ask to stop drinking, or you ask for another drink. It depends on what you need. You are still requesting your creation to come forth to you from the higher frequency. If it is a positive question, "What do I want for my highest good?" you can imagine very easily that you will get it.

Now we will tell you this, Victoria. Why would not the

Creator, the Universe, the Christ frequency want you to be comfortable in a home and without fear of financial worry? Why not? Why not? Why not? That is as valid a request as anything. And when you can say, "I am enjoined with this request, and I affirm that this is true and I am receiving the bounty that I requested," then you will bring that into form through this frequency. You can be creating more than a light body with this frequency.

"I am Word through my intention to bring forth the perfect living space that is affordable to me and is perfect for all my needs. Word I am Word." That is as valid a decree as "Word I am Word through my desire to grow spiritually." We will tell you this. It's much more difficult to engage in a process of spiritual growth when you are scavenging for a meal. When you are scavenging for a meal, you are hungry. When you are full, you can contemplate a little more easily.

Now there is nothing wrong with having an experience of spiritual growth that is a difficult path, and many, many, many people right now are growing rapidly in spirit because what they felt that they had is suddenly no longer there, and their trust in the material has changed. They believed that the job would save them, or that the car would always be in the garage. And now suddenly they may be living in the car that used to drive them to the job that didn't save them. So everybody now is having to look differently.

Now the example that we gave you is a process of spiritualization through difficulty, and that is fine. There are two different ways man can intend to grow spiritually. One is through conscious intention, and one is through getting bounced around enough that one has to go there out of necessity. That is "hitting a bottom," if you wish, or having an experience of being confronted with something that the conscious mind, and the tools that the conscious mind has had to fix it, suddenly fail. So people learn that way all the time and we do not judge it.

To learn through conscious intention is to be engaged in a different process, and that is to say, "I am receptive to my learning and I am on the path and I am going to learn what is required to bring me to where I need to go each step of the way." That does not necessarily mean that the physical reality that you know will remain intact. In likelihood it will not. You may want a different job, or a different house, or a different set of keys to a whole bunch of different houses containing different possibilities at the end of this road. You will not know that until you arrive there. So we say to you, in time this will become clear. But don't denounce your requirements for physical comfort because, in fact, they are there in order to support you in moving forward in other ways as well. Period. Question?

VN: That's good for me now. What about you, Paul?

We want to talk to Paul for a moment about what he creates in his life and how he fears things and how those fears
come into manifestation. For the last two days he's been
frightened about healing issues and that does not mean he
will create illness. However, it does mean that he creates mental constructs that he then has to make so with his conscious
intentions. So we want to give him an exercise to heal the
body of the need to project illness into the future.

"I am Word through my body" claims the body into alignment with Christ. "I am Word through my physical presence"
actually implies that the presence that you are embodied is
actually in the Christ. "I am Word through my future body,"
well, Paul is already saying, "How can that be claimed?" It can
be claimed as follows:

> "I am Word through the body that I inhabit throughout time.
> And any form the body takes in any lifetime is magnificent
> and acclimated to the frequency of the Word. I am Word
> through this intention. Word I am Word."

You are actually engendering, yes, to send a light out forward into the future through this present time that anchors
the vibration of the Christ into physical form and that will
project healing into the physical body. But to focus on disease,
of course, undermines healing. It does not always bring forth
disease, but it sure doesn't make it easy to be in your health.

So we acknowledge this, Paul, and we say to you this: You are healthy, you are healing, you are healed. And you are choosing now to stay in a healed body. "I am Word through this intention. Word I am Word."

Thank you both for this reading today. We are grateful for your attentions. Word I am Word. Thank you and stop.

THREE

RECOGNITION

March 5, 2009

We want to talk today about life and what life is. And life is not a time frame that you exist in. Life is a set of experiences that align you to greater knowing. It is a school, really. It is a time of lessons. And a life is actually an expanse of time that growth can occur in. If you understand this, you take the onus off the fear of achievement in a lifetime, because you understand that this time in life is about learning this thing or that thing, and that these lessons will continue on life after life after life.

This is, in many ways, the opportunity for you to let go of fear about having to be a certain way at a certain time in order to free you up to do things in a way that will teach you. When you are always looking at the goal, you actually bypass the lessons that you were leading to through the effort to arrive there. That's interesting, but it's also not required to focus yourself in such a way that the bypassing of knowledge precludes you from learning the lessons you are intended to learn as you arrive at each stage of growth.

Now we say to you this. The responsibility for your growth, of course, is yours. And the circumstances that you bring forward in your life have been brought forward by you to teach you what you need to know. As you grow forward in time, you understand that you have things that you need to learn and therefore you call to you the circumstances that you need in order to bring that growth and that understanding, that learning, into being. That is always an agreement that you make with yourself, and you do this prior to incarnation with a larger set of lessons that a lifetime, a period of time, will hold for you. And you also do it systematically through an assessment of your progress towards these goals as you go about your life. So we say to you this. "What is life?" is really, "What are the set of experiences that I will bring to me and produce in order to learn the lessons that I came here to learn?" And this is very, very, very simple. So we say to you now, you are in a growth process, and we are deciding now to bypass a program that was set in place by you, by all of you, that this kind of growth towards spiritualization, towards understanding yourself as spirit, would take many lifetimes.

It has taken many lifetimes in order to bring you to where you stand today. You are reading this book, you are hearing this voice, and you are already comprehending that you must be on a path because you are intrigued and you are excited and you are believing the possibility that you can incarnate as yourself at a higher frequency while existing in this life you are living in now. That is the radical message of this teaching, and it is happening today.

So we say to you this. When we say we are bypassing a programming, we are actually intending to bring forth a resolve in your energy system to take the brakes off the car and to speed up a process because this is the time when this can be achieved. Because the energies on the planet lack the density that they did in the past and the requirement of consciousness to change is imperative. This is happening now, this is happening now, this is happening now.

So we say to you this. When we bypass the programming that has been in place that's stated a soul can only go so far in one lifetime, we are being economical, we are doing this in a succinct way to bring about the intended passage in your consciousness that will bring this shift into fruition. You are wondering, Paul, does this mean we are breaking any rules by bypassing this programming?

Absolutely. Yes, we are breaking a rule that states that you must hang around in your consciousness until you believe you can go farther and bring to you those sets of experiences that will acclimate you and bring you to the next level of truth and understanding as the Christ. We are bypassing that intentionally through one octave each week, each moment, each time we bring to you the frequencies that are available to you now on this plane.

You have each decided already prior to incarnation that this would be the lifetime that you would manifest yourself fully in consciousnesses. And while this has retained its memory in your being in a subtle way, many of you only now are waking up to this possibility through the actions of this text and the circumstances that led you to read it. This chain of events has been in place for many years, and this is the time that the chain is opened and inclusive and everyone is coming to it.

Paul is asking for explanation, and what this really means is that the plan for this time to be open to the acclimation of spirit incarnating in man has been planned, has been proceeding, for many, many years. This is not an event that was decided on Tuesday last week when you got on the telephone and discussed this. This was not about anything other than the requirement of consciousness to become one with the Christ manifestation on this plane that has been intended for two thousand years. This is a time of recognition of who you are.

If you ask what led you, on a practical level, to this choice, you will be surprised that the manifestations of coincidence, if you would like to call them that, brought you here with full intention on your part to be in this moment now. The walk to the store that led you here was inspired by a thought you had that was inspired by a conversation or a dream or something, but regardless, you did not just arrive at this bookcase and buy this primer because they did not have the novel you were looking for. This was part of a suggestion that was planted in you by your own consciousness some time ago. And we are not speaking of sales; we are simply talking about what it takes to bring someone to an awareness and readiness of their growth.

If you ask yourself, and if you go back and say, "When did I first realize that I had a calling to understand myself spiritually?" you will understand that that was a suggestion that was imprinted in you, into your consciousness, by your own spirit, by your own Higher Self and those beings that work with you to elevate you in consciousness. That happened a long time ago and the recalling of it will remind you that, in many ways, you have been on this path for years and years and years. Everybody has.

Paul is seeing an image now of a bus station and many, many people gathering at a bus station who have not known one another in the past. But everybody is called here, and everybody is acknowledging that they know one another by recognition if not by name. Everybody has been called to take this trip and everybody gets on the bus. And once they are in the bus, they are in the frequency, and they are traveling.

This is the bus, you are in the frequency, and you are

traveling. Do you understand this? This is not a little thing. This is a huge thing. You are a part of something. You are part of energetic movement and a creation that will have effects and intend to, for a thousand years. This is the next passage of time, this is the next age, this is the next time, and you are part of the heralding and part of the creation that is shifting this on a global level as the consciousness of this plane rises in frequency. And we say this with recognition and with joy that the time has come for man to say, "I am Word. I am Word. I am Word."

Now we want to talk to you now about things that you have been wondering about as you read this primer. And you wonder about worth still, and what that means. What does it mean to be worth yourself? What does it mean to be worthy of the Creator? What does it mean to allow yourself to believe you can have an experience of the self as Word?

We want to offer you something now that will support you in receiving yourself as worthy of this journey. You have purchased the ticket when you bought the book, or when it was handed to you by a friend, or when you believed that you could do this and that you would find the means and the channels to find yourself in the consciousness of the Christ frequency. So you already have some worth, the belief that this can be so, otherwise you would not have read so far. You would not have put up with it. You would have tossed it in the baggage along with the other books that promise things that you do not believe can ever be delivered. And that would be an appropriate thing for you to do if you are at that place of understanding that says, "No." But you are not at that place. You have said, "Yes," and you are on the journey.

So we require you now to take that aspect of the self that believes that she is worthy, that small piece of the self that smiles in recognition to this work, and says, "Yes, this is what I think is so," "Yes, I understand this," and "Yes, I am willing to believe that I can be on this journey." That small aspect of the self now must become enlarged and we are going to do it as follows:

WE WANT YOU TO ENVISION YOUR WORTH AS A DIVINE Being as a speck of light at the core of your being. A golden speck at the heart that believes that she is worthy of her journey to the Christed Self. And we want you to envision this gold spark alighting as a flame. As a very small flame regarding itself beautifully as it catches more light. You are a small fire burning in your heart. And as you do this, you begin to experience heat in the heart center as the flame rises and flickers. And this is your self-worth, this is your own Christed Self in being manifesting as you.

And now you say, "I am worth my journey. Word I am Word." And as you say this, it is as if the flame is risen within your heart and rises in prominence. And the heat regards itself as opening up and beginning to fill the chest as a chamber of fire.

"Word I am Word through my belief that I am worthy of u.
journey of the spirit. Word I am Word. I am Word through
the self-worth that requires me to believe that I am entitled as
a child of God to come into my manifestation as my Christed
Self. Word I am Word through this intention. Word I am
Word."

At this moment in time the flame is burning in your chest
and this is your own worth as a Divine Being made manifest.
This is the aspect of you that is the Christ, and the heart is
burning, aligned to this vibration at this second in time.

Now we want to amplify that light again and allow that
light to become you as Word. And in order to do this, we
require Paul to step back into the scenery, because we are
going to speak some words that he is not familiar with. And
these are the words we will speak:

"I am changing my incarnation and my path to vibrate at one
with my Christed Self. I acknowledge myself as my Divine
Self in full manifestation. I align to the Creator in all ways,
who will support me in bringing forth this frequency fully
and with light to change my being on a level of structure and
form to own myself in consciousness as an aspect of the Creator fully realized, embodied in light. I am now changing the
physical form that I stand in. I am now changing the consciousness that I inhabit and respond to. I am now changing

the alignment I have always held to a higher alignment. And in doing this, I allow myself to become Christed in form.

"I bring to me now the powers and the requirements of this transformation. I call to me now the benefits and the changes of this transformation. I call to me now those beings who will support me in my passage to align me fully to the requirements and to the vestige of this expression as a self incarnating as the Christ. As I do this, I change my name. I am Word, I am Word, I am Word.

"I have become that which I have stated. And in doing so, my recognition of myself as the Creator of my world begins to come into consciousness in a way that I can experience. And my relationship with my Creator, the Great Creator goes into harmonious accord and we work together as one energy vibrating at a frequency of Christ.

"I have transformed my soul. I have made myself new. I have called to me those energies that will transform the nature and being of who I believe I am. And as I do this now, I bring to me the magnitude of light at the highest frequency that my system can realize. And in this moment I merge my light, my own Christed flame with the light that surrounds me, and I intend to become myself in fullness as Word. I am Word through this intention. Word I am Word.

"I am that I am. I am one with Father that created me. I am one with the Universe that I exist in. I am in my Christed

Self. And I experience myself now as energy, as form, as energy, as form, as energy, as form. I am doing this now. I am in transformation. I am in my light and I am worthy of this journey. Word I am Word through this intention. Word I am Word."

Now we want you to stop for a moment and we want to explain what we just did. What we just did was transform your energy frequency into a Christed vibration, and then we merged this energy with the energy of the Creator. And the magnificence of this, in your understanding, and in our understanding, is enormous. And in your change you will now begin to experience yourself as frequency in a manifestation of the Christ in a way that has not been possible while you existed in a physical body.

Now this change has been made. It has been anchored in. And for the next two weeks upon this exercise, you will find yourself magnifying this energy and frequency as you align to it. And your feelings in your body will begin to shift as you become accustomed to existing in a higher frequency. We will give you some examples of what you might expect.

Your body will feel as if it's elongated, as if you are longer than you are. And what is really happening is you are aligning to the higher frequencies that are extending your energy field outward and upward. Your body may ache as you release those things that have impeded your growth that are actually held in physical form. And if this happens, we respond to you with your request for healing by saying, "I am Word through this pain in my leg, or in my heart, or in my vision. Word I am Word."

When you state that intention, "I am Word through this," or "I am Word through that," what you are doing is you are sending the energies to that place and requiring it to be healed in the manifestation of the Christ energy. And to do this does require your willingness and your faith, because if you do it as a mantra but you do not believe it, you will have said some words, but you will have not made a true statement of truth. Anyone can say, "I am [name of a movie star]," and everyone will know you are not that person.

When you state, "I am Word through this intention," you deliver energy to what was intended. When you send energy to an arm or to a leg or to a cell or to a pain, you are doing the same thing. You are setting the intention that the Divine Self that you are sends the energy of the Christ to inform the healing of that which is needed. So the body is going to change, so do not be alarmed if you feel funny sometimes. All you are really doing is acclimating to the higher frequencies.

Now you want to know about your emotions and what will happen there, and this is pause for some real discussion. Your emotional self has been created by your past experience. You all have dispositions. Some of you are depressive. Some of you are always sunny. And whatever those creations have been, they have been appointed by you. You've been much involved with the creation of your personality. You have an enormous vested interest in it. So watching it begin to transform can cause some panic.

Now we do not tell you that you change who you thought you were. We tell you this: you become who you truly are. So if you were a pain in the ass always, you may find that that behavior no longer works and frustrates you and brings you down. And we ask you this: is it okay to continue to affirm that you are Word through your personhood? Because if you say, "Yes," then you have a tool to transform the personality into a higher frequency as well.

But the emotions, that which has had a vested interest in the way things have been through the experience of feeling, "how I feel in a certain position," "when I do a certain thing," or "when a certain this is said to me," that is very habituated behavior. And the work that you're going to have to undergo is realigning the personality to the possibility that it can relinquish things that are no longer serving its purpose.

The personality is willing to heal and transform. The emotional self that has an investment in responses to a certain thing in a habitual way is the one that really has to be taught, because you know yourself through your personality and your emotions show you what you feel. "I am having a bad day because I *feel* terrible. Not because I was yelled at at work, but because I felt terrible when I was yelled at at work." So you have been creating your reality through emotional responses as much as anything else. And the emotions need some work here.

So we're going to give you another exercise to amplify your emotional self and to align it to the Christ frequency.

Your emotional body has requirements in order to recognize itself as who it is. "If I didn't get angry on Mondays, I would not be me." "If I didn't smile when I got a present, I wouldn't be me." "If I didn't feel joy when I watch that television show I like so much, I wouldn't be me." "If I didn't cry when I was sad, I wouldn't be me." All of these ways are ways that you inquire yourself to know yourself through your experience of your feelings. So we will say now that we want to transform the way in which you experience your feelings so that you may recognize them as responses to your external matter and experience and not as who you truly are. There is a difference here, so we will say this to you. We want you to ask the feelings at this time to begin to release the need to control your emotional self in ways that preclude you from realizing yourself in the higher frequency.

And this means this. We are telling you that you are in control of your emotional self. And by giving permission to the emotional self to stop fighting change will actually give you permission to change. And we will do it through this affirmation:

"I am Word through my intention to allow my emotional response and my feeling self to begin to align to the possibility of change. And I require my feeling self to work with me in alignment with the achievement of my resolution to incarnate as my Christed Self. I become aware of myself in response to physical exchanges and experiences and I understand that my feelings, up till now, have been programmed by me to produce certain effects.

"As I align now to the higher frequency, I give permission to these feelings to change and to self-regard in such a way that I may know that I am in choice and have my choice of how I respond to external exchanges and experiences. In doing this, I give myself permission to align my frequency on a feeling and emotional level to the Christed form that I am undertaking to inhabit. I am Word through this intention to realize my feeling self as Word. Word I am Word through this intention. Word I am Word."

Now when we tell you you are intending to align your feeling self as Word, what we are simply saying is this. It is time for you to understand that your feelings are an aspect of the self that you actually can control. And when you align your feeling self to the higher frequency, that self begins to inform how the feelings can change, so that you are not ruled by lower frequencies when you feel frustrated or alarmed or depressed because you will understand that your feelings can be transformed through your intention as much as anything else can. We hope this has made sense to you and we will address it again when we take questions at the end of the session. And yes, Victoria, we are giving you a reminder that there may be questions you would like to ask and we will answer them, as we best are able to.

So today you have actually had a lesson in transformation and merging with the energy of the Christ. So we will give today's chapter a title, which is actually this: "Recognition." That is the title of Chapter 3, "Recognition." And you are recognizing yourself as the frequency of the Word as you move forward and progress through this alchemical process of transformation that you have engaged in.

Now we want to talk to you for a moment about requirements for living and what it means to be aligned to your life path, as you exist in your life. Because the first thing we talked about today was life and what life is. When you have requirements for a life, you have things that you think that you need in order to bypass trouble. So: "I need an accountant to do my taxes." "I need a comfortable home." "I need a boyfriend or girlfriend to go to the movies with." "I need money for my child's education."

These are all practical requirements for a life. But we want to give you another way of looking at it. The requirements for your life at this time, through this channeling and through this engagement with the process of wonder and recognition that you have already undertaken, require your life to transform. The landscape that you exist in requires transformation. You cannot be the new person standing in the old kitchen looking at the old pots and pans that cooked yesterday's dinner. Everything is made new in Christ. That is actually a promise in the Jesus teachings. "Behold, I make things new." This is a promise that you are now in as well.

Now the kitchen that you stand in with yesterday's pots are still there, but they will be perceived anew. And then you will have to decide whether you want to wash your pots, replace your pots, or move to a new city where you have new pots or no pots at all. Your changes will be made clear to you through your own vocation, through your own knowing, through your own requirements for the life that you will live once you have changed into yourself more fully. There is nothing to be done today but transform. But the process of transformation and integration is a deep and profound one. And this changes where you go and what you do.

We will talk now about the requirements for where we will go. This change that you change and become will make you anointed and your frequency will be high enough that that which you encounter will begin to transform by your nature and by your proximity to it. And what this means very simply is, you will become an energy field that impacts the energy fields of those things and those beings that you will encounter.

When something no longer resonates with you at the high

frequency, you will find that it falls away, it cannot be held, and it will be replaced by something that actually resonates at a frequency that it is in alignment to. This is very important for you to understand. It's why suddenly the relationship that you are in may seem empty. And while you may love the being that you have chosen to stand beside, you will realize that you no longer resonate with him, or the job that you are in, or the kitchen you stand in, or the path that you have chosen for yourself out of duty and obligation and not out of wisdom and creation and joy. All of these things may begin to transform as you acclimate to the Christ frequency in fullness.

And we are going to encourage you, at this time, to begin to experience yourself in your life and see what areas begin to feel uncomfortable, like an itchy sweater, or a "downer," or a past habit that no longer brings to you the comfort that you used to regain from re-creating the same behavior again and again.

If I already sit in the same chair to watch my television show or read my magazine and that chair starts feeling uncomfortable, that would be a small indicator. If I suddenly look at my job and wonder why I am still here, that is another indicator. If I suddenly realize that I have a joy to do something new and I am being encouraged by my soul's purpose to investigate that joy, I had best to start investigating.

So you may start growing things. Or you may start looking

for other work that suits you in your new place of being. Or you may find that a new partner makes himself available to you through this Christ consciousness and that you will resonate differently with his response than you have with your previous engagements. Period.

All of these things may happen, or else you will resist, and then you will have a different kind of discomfort through the resistance. "If I'm not going to change and I'm going to hold tight to what I know," you're actually going to feel restless and angry. And restlessness and anger are two indications that you are blocking this process. So your feelings can actually contribute to your understanding of what this process really is, when you mark it as such. Period.

So if you feel uncomfortable doing what you've always done, or you are in an engagement that suddenly feels uncomfortable and you resist moving beyond it, then you will have teachers through your emotional experience coming to you to support you in the changes that you need to make.

We want to talk about something else for a few moments before we take your questions. And Paul was wondering last night about the requirement of forgiveness. What does man do when man believes himself not to have been forgiven by himself, or by his Creator, or by his fellow man? What is the process of forgiveness? Is one really required to forgive his enemies in order to ascend in consciousness?

We will tell you this: It's actually not possible to ascend in consciousness to the extent that you require your brother to suffer. It is not possible to rise in frequency when you hold the lower frequency to your heart and refuse to release it. And unforgiveness, of course, is a lower frequency.

However, there has been some misunderstanding around this issue, and we would like to try to rectify it a bit today in this teaching. To unforgive is to block forgiveness. The natural state of man is to be in forgiveness and the recognition of the divinity of his brother. That is actually the true state of who you are and how you are intended to negotiate with one another and behave with one another and experience one another. It's as if the dance was always in place and everybody could step on one another's foot as part of the dance and not be smacked for it. And somewhere along the road, man began to hold grudges and to covet and to fear and consequently began to hold their brothers outside of the light while claiming that they could be in the light. And isn't that an impossibility, to stand in the light while you demand your brother stand in the darkness?

Now unforgiveness, as we have just stated, is the blocking of forgiveness. So we want to unblock you now and unblock any unforgiveness that you may be holding to the self and to the fellows, or to the self and against the Creator. Many of you have great rage at what you believe God to be, because he has taken things from you, or you believe he has, when in fact, of course, God does not take, God gives. God is the benefactor, and creation has its cycles of life and death and transformation. So blaming God never gets you anywhere except angry. And sometimes anger can support you and create an understanding of your own power and your own worth. But just as often, it blocks you from the flow of your own Divine Self. Because your own Divine Self actually works at a higher frequency and doesn't really get angry about anything. It's gotten over it already, as it were. So we want to do some unblocking of forgiveness right now.

> "At this moment in time, I am choosing to forgive myself for any and all trespasses I may have incurred against myself and my fellow man and my Creator. I am willing to be forgiven for any and all beliefs that I have held that have stopped me from experiencing myself as forgiven by my Creator. I am now allowing myself to believe that I can be, and that I am, and that I am being forgiven for anything and everything that I may have done, that I may have imagined, that I may have thought, that I may have experienced, that I may have chosen or that I may have been gifted with that has given me reason not to forgive myself, my Creator, and my fellows. I am now free of unforgiveness and I stand firm in my knowing that I am worthy of the Creator and that I am worthy of my fellow man, and I am worthy of the journey I intend to go on in my Christed Self. I am Word through this intention. Word I am Word."

We are saying now that unforgiveness is merely a mechanism that keeps you in place. It locks you in and it locks the relationship into a dynamic that actually does not move. The relationship cannot transform when unforgiveness is in play. So the easiest thing to do in order to forgive is to allow it to be and simply state:

> "The willingness to forgive this person or this situation is present within me through the Christ presence that I am inhabiting. Word I am Word through this intention. Word I am Word."

And then let this alignment come to pass. Period. That's right, it will come to pass. You have to encourage it only by deciding that you are not going to continue to withhold forgiveness against your fellow, or the situation, or the self or the Creator. That much is in your hands to make so.

Now we want to stop and we want to tell you something, that the next chapter is about understanding and love, and we want to open you up now to understanding and love in preparation for the chapter that is to come. If you would affirm this:

> "As I stand in my Christed energy and in my higher frequency, I open now to understanding and I open now to the frequency of love. As I experience myself in my understanding

and in my love, I align to the cosmic understanding of great truth and the truth of my being as a divine soul incarnating as my Christed Self. As I stand here in this understanding, I know myself as loved and I become part of the frequency of love that is available to me through this intention. I am choosing now to stand in my love, to stand in my understanding, and I am Word through this intention. Word I am Word."

Receive your love now. And receive this through your energy field. Feel the energy around you begin to transform as you stand, as you sit, as you are wherever you are. The energy around you right now, which is our energy and which is the energy of the Creator within you working in tandem, is aligning you now to the frequency of love through your understanding and we welcome this as part of your passage.

For the next day you may feel that there is a tingling and a frequency elevation around you, and we will benefit you with this, as we are able. Just understand that this is your own system, your own energy field, beginning to align to the higher frequency. You do not need to feel alarmed. You can actually enjoy it. You are safe, you are protected, you are being worked with by those on our side who are facilitating the growth of being within you and with all the readers of this text. We have a small brigade whose job it will be to shift you as you need to be shifted and you can call on us by name.

"I am now calling on those who work in the frequency of the Word from the Divine Light to come to me and to support me in my transformation. And I ask to know them in my frequency through their feelings of love for me. I am Word through this intention. Word I Word."

Thank you both. We will stop now.

FOUR

LOVE AND UNDERSTANDING

March 6, 2009

We are ready for the work to start. Corrections are being made in your energy systems as a result of the work that you have been doing. And when we say corrections, what we mean is that the aspects of the self that are no longer serving you are being addressed individually. And these things, of course, hang out in your energy fields and then amplify and create problems when they are activated. These are things like problematic thinking, or behaviors, or stuck energies that manifest in ways that do not support you and out-picture themselves in your life as problems. So that is being addressed through this work that we have commenced with you, the reader, through the amplifications of this text as they are imprinted in your frequency, in your Christed Self, through your journeying forward.

We said yesterday that we would speak to you about understanding and what understanding is. And understanding actually is a way of knowing and a process of knowing, but it is not knowing. And once you come to knowing on a deeper level, the process of understanding is changed. You may actually find that as you move forward, what you thought you thought, what you think you think, and what you believe you understood will be changed because you will know. And as you know, the constructs that have been created through false belief systems, through false understanding, through false identity, through your thought processes will dismantle and then you are left with the truth that was underneath it all along.

You wonder what we mean. We will give you an example. If you have always believed that you were a certain way and that truth that you have existed in was actually based in a misperception, once that misperception is cleared all of the behaviors that have been created in response to it will have to go away. And what you are left with, finally, is the real deal, that which lay underneath. And in this case, the best example we can give you is that you are the Christed Being and that the false self that has been made prominent is actually in the process of release.

So those constructs of personality are actually clearing at this time, one at a time, in ways that you can work with. We have restated this because it will be helpful to you through this next passage.

We are going to ask Paul to step back again so that we can

work with him more fully to bring you the information you require. Let God take over this correct channeling session. "I am Word through this intention. Word I am Word."

They are saying, "Receive hand on heart." Everyone, please, in your imagination at this time imagine that a hand is being placed on your heart center and the energies coming through this hand are the energies of the Creator. And the heart is now aligning to the vibration of the Word. And as it does so, your heart explodes in a beautiful light and a flame of the Creator that burns within you.

We ask you now to receive yourself as loved. And what we do is invite the energy field that you exist in to integrate with the energies of love that are present for you at this time. So we will bring the energies through you now and align you to them in fullness.

"I am Word through my availability to receive love. Word I am Word through this intention. Word I am Word."

Now the energy field that you are in is beginning to transform itself, and this has been a process that was begun with this text on one level and on other levels has been present and operational since you were first incarnated in your first lifetime on this plane. You have always been in process, but what we are giving you now is an integration of an aspect of the Creator that can be made into flesh. And part of this accommodation for you is the requirement that you begin to integrate with the energies of love.

Now why, do you ask, is love an aspect of this Creator? When you understand love in its true sense, you will begin to experience it to the level that you can commit to. In most cases, you are still informed by the limitations that you have embellished the construct of love to be. It is not a pair of shoes. It is not the great apartment. It is not even the boyfriend or the child that you say you love. Love is a manifestation of the Creator that works with people, that works through vibration to call forth the action of God. And the action of God is the Word. So you cannot be without love when you are in the action of transforming the Word, the self, into the Creator's frequency, and that is what is happening here. So love, we say to you, is a manifestation of the Creator that can be worked with. But at the same time you must believe that the self can be loved in fullness.

And now we want to work with you directly on your love. When you say, "I love someone," you actually can mean it, but at the same time you are still approving of it on a conscious level as if that is a decision. "I choose to love my husband," or "I love my husband because he is my husband," or "I love Max, or Seymour, or Angelica," or name the name. In any case, you believe on a certain level that you are the one in charge of the love when in fact, of course, that is not the case.

The God Self, the aspect of the self that is God, is the lover within you and to the extent that you decree that this love is exchanged and has to have a return invested in it, you do not really love. If you say, "I love the postman" to the extent that you say, "I love the husband," you are getting more on the right track. Because we actually say to you, true love is not a condition. It is a frequency that is emitted that transforms that which it encounters. And it is free and it is not to be dictated as much as it is to be expressed.

When you are a transmitter for the higher frequencies, which is what you are, your energy field becomes a tuning fork, and when you are attuned to the frequency of love, the energy of love works with you and through you to make itself known. If you are working with this still as a personality construct which intends to love someone in a special way because you choose it, you may be in an aspect of love, but you are not in the experience of love as much as the illusion of love. And there is indeed a difference.

The illusion of love is a personality construct that has requirements attached to it. The belief of love as a personality construct has been a problem here for a very long time. People divorce when they fall out of love. And, in fact, falling in love is an experience of love, but it is an embellishment of love and it is not a truth in the higher sense. The truth of love moves through the system and makes itself embellished in a truthful way. It does not commit other than to say, "I am in love." To be in love means, truly, to be in the frequency of love and not to be in the construct of love that has requirements. We believe we are making sense.

But everyone here who has a belief in love still holds firm to the possibility that it will become what they intended it to be. Now we are not going to discount romance and the benefits of it as an enlightening experience into the frequency of love. But true love lasts beyond the fall into love. True love extends itself perfectly into the Christ frequency because if you can understand this, then you will understand that the Christ frequency is a love energy made manifest through you. And when it is made manifest through you, it has an action, and that is to love.

When you are in judgment of another for any reason, you distort your perceptions of that person and you step out of the Christ consciousness and you move out of love. When you can understand truthfully that the frequency of love implies love without any sense of judgment at all, then you will begin to move through this in an active way that is experiential to you.

Now we give you exercises that will support you in your understanding of love.

Imagine right now that you stand on a street corner and you see people pass by you and you see them in their worth as a Created Being. You can understand this. There is a Creator and he made everybody, so consequently everyone must have some worth attached to him or her and you bear witness to this. So you see yourself standing on the corner, watching people pass, and you acknowledge that they are all a Created Being.

This is step one in consciousness. You have to do this today as you take your walk, as you sit in your school, or your office, or your apartment and you greet your neighbor. You greet your neighbors with the acknowledgment that they are a Created Being and created by the Creator who makes Himself known through his creations. You do this with the intention to observe your own responses. "Where am I judging? Why am I judging? How do I feel when I acknowledge that everyone before me is a creation of the higher frequency of the Creator manifested in form?" This is step one.

Now you will stay there on your corner and you will intend this:

"I am now intending to lift in my frequency where I can benefit from the higher perspective of each man and woman created in the image likeness of their Creator. And I can see them as perfect beings manifested in perfection by the love of the Creator."

And now what you do is you stand on your corner, and with the intention, "Word I am Word to lift my consciousness and vibration to witness the Christ in all that pass me, the Self as the Creator embodied," you will begin to have a different experience. You will begin to see your fellows as perfect creations, perfect creations regardless of what they present in form. The body and the personality construct are fake in comparison to the divine energy that they have incarnated as. And when you are witnessing them in their perfection, you are bypassing all judgment and lifting to your vision as the Christ.

> "I set this intention now. I am seeing all before in the image and likeness of God. I am seeing the Christ in all of my fellows. I am witnessing the divine perfection that is created in every man and woman that I encounter."

When you move to this level of identification, you resonate at a high frequency. And when you resonate at this frequency, you align yourself to the Christ consciousness. And when you are in the Christ consciousness, that which you experience is transformed through the intention to witness the world with the eyes that benefit from the truth of the knowing that God is in everything and everyone and cannot be otherwise. Do you understand this? This is the witnessing of the Creator in your fellows that must be achieved in order to move to the highest level of consciousness available to you now.

Now we will tell you this. In order for this to happen, you have to witness the self as perfect as well. You have to understand that the constructs that you have created that you believe to be limitations, or embarrassments, or faults, or problems that you hold to, keep you from accepting yourself as the truth of what you are, which is the higher frequency incarnated in physical form, so we want to work with you right now to shift this once and for all. Now say this, please:

> "I am Word through my intention to realize myself as my perfect being incarnate. And I stand now before my fellow man and I allow myself to be seen as perfect, as a perfect creation manifested in a body. And I do this now with the support and with the guidance of the powers, the teachers, and the guides that are supporting me on this journey. I do this with the intention to be made manifest as myself as the frequency of the Christ. I am Word through this intention. Word I am Word."

We stand by you now and we support you. And what we are doing with you right now is witnessing you in your perfection. We are seeing you in your perfection, in your perfect body in your perfect spirit, in your wonder. And we are believing you when you say, "I am Word."

We give you an anointing now. And we will do this with an energy that we will call love. And we are going to bless you now in the frequency of love. Receive this through the crown chakra now and let it enfold you.

"I am Word through my being. Word I am Word.

I am Word through my vibration. Word I am Word.

I am Word through my knowing of myself as Word. Word
   I am Word."

When you decree this, you bring yourself into alignment
with the frequency of the Christ. When you set the intention
to become yourself as the Christ consciousness, you elevate
the frequency of the body and the energy field. When you
do this and you intend to witness everyone else as their own
Christ consciousness made manifest, you bless them. So we
will give you this one now:

"I am Word through those I see before me. Word I am
Word."

When you do this, you become a transmitter for the higher
frequency that is working through you and you bring those
before you into an alignment with the Christ consciousness.
You are doing this on a level of energy and they may feel it,
but they will experience it on a higher level and they will be
transformed by it. What you are doing to them and for them
is giving them permission on a higher level to incarnate on
their soul's highest level available to them. That is a promise.

Now when we say this, we do not mean that you are conjuring, or that you are making magic, or you are doing anything

other than witnessing their perfection. And when you say, "I am Word," through someone else, what you are actually doing is aligning them to the resonance of the frequency we call Word, and then that energy becomes imprinted and available to them to work with more actively. Everything operates, simply said, on a level of resonance, and when you are resonating at the higher frequency, you bring those around you into the frequency with you and this blesses them perfectly.

When you understand that you can do this, and that you are doing this, regardless of what you feel, you will understand who you are as energy. If you are having a crappy day and you walk around in crappy energy, no one wants to be around you because you're crappy, because you feel bad, and they bring you down. When someone says something brings them down, they are actually saying the truth. Their energy frequency is being diminished by that which they are encountering. When they are lifted in frequency, they are benefiting, and everyone wants to be lifted. So when you incarnate as yourself in the higher frequencies, you are of benefit to all that you encounter. You are a gift and you are doing work with them on a frequency level regardless of what you intend.

If you walk into a room with the intention of vibrating as the Word, your intention will be met by the frequencies of everyone that you encounter. They may say, "No," on a higher level, and that is their choice, because what we do is not invasive. But what you are truly doing in a frequency level is giving them permission to resonate at this frequency that you are now listening and vibrating and being at. And this tone that you are can be met by them with a wonderful sound: "Yes, yes, yes, yes, yes. I feel this on a level that I may not know, but I can vibrate at this level, too, and in doing so I lift my frequency, and that which has impeded me from my own soul's choice to manifest and incarnate as my Divine Self will be healed. I am doing this now unconsciously, but my frequency knows what it is doing." That is the experience of those you encounter when you are in this energy.

We want to bring you back to the street corner now where we left you standing earlier and you set this intention:

> "I am Word through my being. Word I am Word. I am vibrating in the energy of the Word. Word I am Word. I am manifesting myself as the Word incarnate."

Now you set the intention for those you see before you:

> "I am Word through all those I see before me. I am Word through their experiences of themselves. I am Word through their beliefs. I am Word through their light. I am Word through their requirements for healing."

These are all gifts that can be given freely and in love.

> "I am Word through those before me."

Every week when Paul convenes with his group, they manifest the frequency of the Word with the intention to Word through those before them. When they do this, as you will do this, they bring their frequency to a higher octave and the manifestation of God within them, the energy field that they are, which now vibrates at a high frequency, meets and greets and blesses the energy frequencies of everyone else that has gathered. And this can be experienced in physical ways. We are not speaking metaphorically. When you Word through someone, you can feel the energy and they can feel the energy as well. This becomes part of an attunement. And as you continue to work with frequency, you become better and better at defining and understanding the experience of it.

Paul wants to give you an example now, and we will allow it. When he works with healing and different energies release from the body, they have a different feeling. Fear releases from the body in certain ways, as does anger, as does grief, as does pain. Everything has a torque to it and can be experienced. It is only through the process of encountering the energies again and again that he is able to understand when someone is leaving and releasing a frequency of pain, because he feels the pain that releases on a vibrational level.

This is not unique. You all do this in your own way. When you are feeling badly and you are emitting a certain frequency, you have a tendency to want to hibernate, or hide, or be in your own energies in a way until you feel refreshed and renewed. If you walk into a room where there has been a big fight, you feel the residue of the big fight in the air. It hangs out. That is released energy.

When you have an experience with someone and you say, "That made me feel dirty," the reason is is that you were "slimed," for lack of a better word. They dumped their energy on you in an emotional way and you have a desire now to clean it out. You jump in the shower. You do something to clear yourself out. When you have had a bad night with someone, you want to change the sheets. That is because you are clearing energy. You are all doing this every day, in your way, unconsciously. But your energy field knows what it is doing and it continues to do it anyway, so we are simply making you conscious of energy and how it is so that you can understand it.

We say to you this. The extent that you can witness the Christ, the God within man, is the extent that you can become the Christ incarnate. The real incarnation of the Christ is made known to you through your experience. This is not intellectual, this is experiential, and if your experience does not begin to reflect the higher frequencies, you are missing something, or something was not transcribed properly in this text. But we assure you, we are taking every precaution to inform you of this work in the ways that are cleanest, clearest, and most appropriate for the learning that is required by you. We say this is experiential. You have to experience it.

So you have an assignment today, which is to stand on a corner, or sit in your office or your classroom, and we want you to witness the perfection that is created in every man and woman you see before you. We give you this, and we give you this with a support system, so that you can do this with energy frequencies available to you.

"I am Word through my intention to witness the perfection of every man and woman and child I see before me. I am Word through this intention. Word I am Word."

When this is stated, you bring the frequency into the alignment that will support this transformation of what you see. But you have to choose it, you have to choose it in consciousness, and you have to do it with the intention to see the perfection in those who present themselves to you. Period. That is clearing the fear of being seen as well. The extent that you can witness it in another is the extent that you can begin to believe that you can be perceived this way as well.

Now we want to talk about love again, and when you do this with the intention to see the perfection, you are acting from a place of love, because you are operating out of judgment and judgment is fear in a disguise. Everything you judge you fear. Think about it. Everything you judge you fear. Ask yourself what you judge, and then ask yourself why you fear, and you will know this in your heart once and for all. Everything you judge you fear. And everything you judge you fear because you have an investment in a certain way of thinking, feeling, believing, or a belief that your safety and your personality self is being challenged by it in some way. So we will work on this:

"I am now setting the intention to release any and all judgment of my fellow man, of myself, of anything and everything I perceive in judgment to be released now in perfect ways to bring me into alignment with the Christ expression of truth. I do this willingly and with the understanding that I am protected and safe in my new realization of the perfection I witness before me. Word I am Word through this intention. Word I am Word."

Now we will tell you, to discern something is not to judge it. If I discern that this is not a movie that I will like, I am not saying, "That's a terrible movie." If I am discerning that this is not the right teacher for me, or this is not the right class, or this is not the right job, I am discerning, I am not judging.

We want you to stay in your discernment. To the extent that you don't, you give your authority away and that is a recipe for disaster. You must stay in choice, and to stay in choice you must stay in discernment, otherwise how do you know what to do? So we are not taking away discernment, we are simply telling you that to the extent that you judge your fellow man, you actually lower your own frequency. And when you lower your own frequency, you fall out of alignment with the Christ vibration that you are now working in. You can get back there. You can raise your frequency. But to the extent that you hold another in contempt or in judgment or as less than you, you deny them their own expression as the Christ.

How could you believe that a Creator could favor one man over another? How could you possibly believe that God's love is sanctioned—one is approved of, one is not? You are all perfect creations, you are all deeply loved, and the realization of this, truthfully, will and would transform this planet in a second if it were realized in its fullness. You are all loved. You are all perfect in your expression. We are simply reminding you of who you have always been. Period.

We say this to you now. We said this chapter was going to be love and understanding, and in fact it is. But it is also the call to action now. It is time in the evolution of this journey and the progress of this text to send you out to have an experience of yourself as Christ. So you do this today:

"I stand now in my frequency as the Christed soul that I am. I affirm I am in my frequency as Word and I witness the perfection of all I see before me. Word I am Word through this intention. Word I am Word."

We ask you now to select one person in your life that you can sit with, and we ask that you resonate in the frequency of Word when you are with them. "I am Word through my vibration. Word I am Word." Feel this, please. Do it now. "I am Word through my vibration. Word I am Word." Feel the energy around you begin to lift. Feel this, please. You are doing it. We are aware. You are being worked with. "I am Word in my vibration."

And then we ask that you stand before your friend and witness them as the Word: "I am Word through the one I see before me, Word I am Word. I am Word through the one before me. Word I am Word." When you do this, you transmit the frequency of the vibration of the Word through you and to their frequency. You merge as the gift of the Christ is given, and that happens through intention and that happens on a level of frequency that you can feel and that they will experience. So you do this with them and you ask them, "What did you feel?"

"I am Word through my heart," brings energy to the heart. "I am Word through my liver, Word I am Word," brings energy to the liver. "I am Word through my circumstances," brings energy to your circumstances, but in a way that is general. So the more specific you are with your intention to Word, "I am Word through my hands and feet," "I am Word through my toothache," "I am Word through the one I see before me," the easier it is for you to begin to experience the movement of the frequency through you and to you.

Now we want to say something important. And we said it

last night when Paul convened his class, but it must be understood. You are not the Word as much as you are an aspect of the Word and the energy of the Word moves through you. It is not your ego self. Your personality is not the Word. You do not fix somebody through your ego or through the use of your own energies. The energies work through you because you have become attuned to them and because you are vibrating at a frequency that is high enough to align you to the vibration of the Word. So you are an amplifier and you are a transistor and a receiver of the Creator. The Christ energy works through you. You are a vessel.

If you forget this and you begin to think that you are Jesus or that you are having an identity crisis and have to go join a monastery because your ego is telling you you are special, stop it now. That is not the point of this journey. To the extent that you invest in special-ness, to the extent that you begin to believe that you are the vehicle and the energy that runs the car, you will have problems. You may be the car, you may be the vehicle, but the gas that runs the car is the higher frequency that comes through you.

We hope you understand this. It's an important distinction and we do not want people working with their own energy in ways that will be detrimental to them. An example of this would be, "I am going to heal my cousin Mike of his problem and I am going to Word through it until I do it." You are assuming right then and there that you have control over your cousin Mike, over his malady, and over his choices at a soul level, and you do not.

When you Word through someone, you gift them with the frequency and you allow the frequency to go where it is required in order to do the work that is needed. You can intend to Word through someone's bad knee and trust that you are sending healing, but in fact, you do not do this on an ego level, and if you invest in that healing on an ego level, you are actually blocking the frequency of the energies that are available to you, because you think it's you on a personality level that is doing the work.

You are simply the vehicle for the transformation that is occurring. We do not dismiss this. We do not say this is little. You are honored through your work, but you are worked with and you are worked through. You are your consciousness, and your consciousness is your energy frequency. Understand this. And your energy frequency is connected to a field, a grid that is aligning itself on a much, much, much higher level than has ever been present on this energy field, on this dimensional plane before. The planet is in its own shift and you are part of the shift. Period.

So get out of the way, allow yourself to be who you are in truth: "I am the Word, I am the Word, I am the Word. I am an aspect of the Creator made flesh, as are all men." Period.

So you have an assignment today, and that is to take the

Word out into your own experience and let it be experiential. You will do this. You will take notes. You will write notes to yourself and you will exchange information with the partner that you've chosen to Word through. This will be helpful to you. As you get used to the energies, it will become easier and easier for you to discern what they are.

When Paul shifts, he feels someone and what they are feeling in an empathic way. You will begin to do this as well through your frequency. Information is exchanged through auras all the time. Ninety-nine percent of your exchanges with your fellows are done on a nonverbal level. It's why you feel violated when someone steps too close. They are in your space and your space is your frequency. When you know you love someone, you'd better believe that they know you are loving them as well, because on a frequency level they feel it. It's why you know when someone is lying. It's less about the behavior than it is about the frequency. You are already attuned. We are simply giving you a vocabulary that you can begin to work with to discern, to discern, to discern your own experience. And we said "discern" three times because that is an important piece of this lesson today. You do not judge, you discern.

"I am Word through my being." Affirm this. "Word I am Word. I am Word through my vibration. Word I am Word. I am Word through my knowing of myself as Word."

This is the attunement. Do it as much as you like. Each

time you attune, you bring the frequency of the Word to you and through you in a way that you will begin to experience energetically at a higher and higher level. And as you do this, it becomes easier and easier to discern frequencies in a general sense. We thank you for your work today and we will convene again tomorrow with the next lesson. You are partaking of the lessons and we support you as you do. Word I am Word.

Thank you, goodnight.[1]

---

[1] At the end of this and a few later chapters, the guides said "Goodnight" even though the local time for Paul and Victoria was midday or morning. Asked about this, they replied that it was an appropriate way to finish the session.

FIVE

BOULDERS

March 7, 2009

We're going to work today on thinking and what thinking is. And thinking is a manifestation of what has gone on before you came here, what is going on presently, and what is going on tomorrow. Now we couldn't be much more abstract than that. So we're going to go backwards a step and say, as you know, thoughts are creative and you are creating your reality through your thought processes. And as you do this, you create your reality. That is now understood by many, many people and we are grateful that that has been the news. But we don't understand, then, why so many people continue to create through thinking that supports them in the negative. And by negative we mean it gives them outcomes that are not supporting them in the way that they say that they mean. So when we said your thinking is a product of the past, of the present, and the future, we are not lying to you.

Now you can only think a thought in present time. It can only happen in this moment that you create thought. And your thinking in this present moment is in support of your environment, your relationships; everything that you see before you in many ways has been supported and supported in creation by your thinking. You have chosen it. So you say, "Why do I have this place that I exist in that gives me so much trouble?" or "Why do I own a house when I really want a trailer?" Or vice versa.

Whatever the thought is, you first must understand that this was created by you, through you, based on history. And history is when we say, "the creation of the past." You have a thought in the past, it creates something for you, it becomes part of your world, and then that becomes the basis of future thinking. Because you have manifested something once with a certain thought and had an outcome, good or bad, that is what you based your next experience on. Do you understand this? So you're always building a bridge towards the next phase of your life, to the next action of your life, with your thoughts. Period.

When you say to yourself, "I want something new," and then you continue with the old thought patterns that have supported you in the past, you continue to create what you had. You continue to get what you said you didn't want because you are still producing the same energy system in frequency that will attract to you those very things that are giving you trouble.

So we want to say to you this. How you think is, of course, something that you can take into account and work with on a conscious level. But we will also say if this was as easy as it sounds, everybody would be very wealthy and much happier. So when we talk about your thinking in the past, we are actually talking about those things that have become so rooted that you identify them as you. We have spoken about this already, but it is time now to address them very directly so that you can move past actively creating pain in your lives. Period.

We say pain because we mean pain. You create things in your life with an intention: "I'm going to have a new job because I need more money." "I'm going to get a date because then I will not be alone." And you have these practical aspects of the self that you continue to manifest through your intention. Now your thinking, of course, is the basis for your creations. And when you say something in the form of a decree—"I am this thing," "I am this or that kind of a person," "I am creating this or that"—you are in charge of what you are creating on a very practical level.

But the dismantling of the patterning that creates pain is a substantial undertaking. We are seeing a scaffolding right now up against the face of a building. This is the image that we are imprinting in Paul's consciousness, in his mind's eye. And there are workmen on the face of the building that is currently under renovation. And this is actually you, right now. You are under renovation. And the workmen are working.

And now when we talk about pain, we want to tell you this. We cannot do cosmetic work. We have to go right in there and pull the stuff out that is creating so many problems for you. If we were to tell you that you could go on this journey and not have to deal with your pain in a very direct way, we would not be serving you in the least, and we would be full of it. Because you would be told that you were getting pabulum, that you were getting the easy ride through invocation, that you were being told that you can banish your pain by conjuring some words and then ignoring it.

Well, you are not conjuring words when you do an invocation of the Christ energy by affirming, "I am Word," you are actually trading the lower frequency for the higher one, and that creates an alchemical response of bringing the higher frequency in, in a way that can support you in your changes. But it is not abracadabra, nor is it a way out from facing your truth.

When you embark on any path of spiritual growth, you have to be willing to say to yourself, "What stands in the way of my appointment with my Divine Self in creation must be cleared." That is a mandate.

Now you can actually live in a room for a very long time

with a boulder in the center of the room that you ignore. That is the elephant in the living room for some people. But we prefer a boulder because a boulder is big, it sits there, and you actually create a whole life around this boulder. You move your furniture around it. You sit behind it. It blocks things. But you take it for granted that that boulder is there and will stay there and your whole life has been supported by its presence.

What we will tell you is this. When that boulder is out of the room, there is a whole lot more light available to you. There is a whole lot more energy and there is a whole lot more of you that can be expressed as your Divine Self in action.

So we will give you some examples of what boulders are. Boulders are creations. They are creations that you have either inherited culturally, or that you have created by yourself, or that you have decided you have to have for some reason in the past that may have made perfect sense when it was created, but it is now an obstruction of great magnitude. And we must clear it.

So we will say what a boulder is is an obstruction in your consciousness. A false belief that has engendered other energies to attach to it and creations to the extent that it has become very, very large and now you take it for granted and you assume it must always be there because you misinterpret it and believe that it is you. And it is you, to the extent that you have created a life that supports it.

So an example of a boulder would be, "Men are terrible," and guess what? If you believe that, that all men are terrible, they are. And that is your experience. If you believe that you can never have a lot of money because if you do it will be taken from you, or people will be angry at you, or that it will be a detriment to your spiritual growth to have things that give you pleasure, you have created a boulder. And all of these things sit in your living room, which is your consciousness, and take up a lot of space and create your experience in this life. So how do you get rid of a boulder? It's not like taking out the trash. It has to be dismantled and cleared and we will say transmuted by the Christ light.

Now first of all, you are used to a process that says, "Everything must be hard. Everything must take years. I need to go to the therapist and talk about this for a long time to find out why I created my boulder. And then I have to get rid of it. And I'm gonna do it with a toothpick and pick away at it until maybe it goes away. But I don't really believe it's gonna go, because I'm actually very attached to it." This is the process that you engage in culturally around transformation. You all believe it's an arduous undertaking.

Now earlier in this chapter we said it's not going to be abracadabra. A magic wand is not going to come down and tap on your boulder three times and get it out of the room. But what we are going to tell you is this. It does not need to be dismantled through an extended process that requires that you hold, hug, embrace, touch, examine, and self-identify as your boulder. That's a bunch of junk at this point and we want you to understand why.

To the extent that you create a problem and then you maintain a relationship with a problem as a living thing, as "my problem that I have to contend with," you continue to create the problem. And you continue to add ammunition and impact and structure to that very thing you say you are trying to clear up, and this is cultural at this stage of the game.

In the old days, people believed in miracles. And when you have a miracle, you can have one that happens in an instant or over a long period of time. It doesn't really matter. But the energies that you contend with these days tend to be of a density that is much more difficult to create the kind of alchemy that would clear a boulder in a second. But we are going to do it pretty quick, and we promise you this.

Now we are not doing it. You are going to do it. And you are going to choose one thing today that you want to clear and clear once and for all in the Christ frequency that we claim as Word. You are going to do this with an intention to decide, once and for all, that it is your divine right to be without this thing that has created your pain, or that you give power to in such a way that it creates your pain.

Now if you do this, and you do this from a higher place,

which is a place of affirmation that you have the right to be without this thing, you can actually begin to clear it. But the first thing you have to do is believe firmly that it can be healed, that it can be cleared, and that you are the one who is working with it actively to be in this pattern of clearing. Period.

Now when you say, "I am Word through this thing that I identify as my pain," you are bringing the Christ frequency to the energy that has been created in pain, and that begins to work on the pain. Now Paul is seeing an image in his mind's eye of a boulder that is beginning to shimmer in a light frequency, and that is a start, but that is not necessarily going to dismantle the boulder.

The boulder itself is a creation. And there are many aspects to creation other than one thought. For example, your belief that you are unattractive may have been compounded by your mother and your friends and what you see on television and what your culture believes. And so the pain that you feel around your visual self, or how you are perceived, is a big deal because it's reflected back at you every time you feel ashamed or ugly or unloved, or every time you see an image that reminds you of what you feel about your physical self. Do you understand what we are saying?

Now we say it's compounded by a lot of thoughts, but the thoughts in the past that have created this can be cleared in the present and we are not going to do microscopic surgery

on this boulder. We are going to blast it, as it were, and transmute it. But to understand, first of all, that there are many
things that contribute to the creation of a large pattern of
pain, and that is the reason most people don't know how
to address it in consciousness. It's not as simple actually as
just going back to a time when something was created. That
works, and we gave you examples of that, but what we do say
is that going back to that time with an understanding that
there have been add-ons and other ways that the pattern has
become cemented will show you that when you work on this,
you have to work on it in several levels.

The first level is the creation of the pain:

"I choose this one thing now that I am going to undertake
to clear from my consciousness once and for all and I am
going to affirm this: In my intention to release this pattern of
[fill in the blank], I am now willing to undertake the exercise
that follows. In this work I will become actively engaged in
the focus and responsibility of my own healing through my
understanding that it is my will in alignment with the will
of my Creator that supports me in choosing to release that
which creates my pain.

"I do this now with the understanding that I will have to
see the pain that I am releasing and I must address it clearly
and with light. I do this now with the intention to remove

myself from the role of victim that may perpetuate this pattern and give me solace on any level. I affirm that I am releasing any blame attached to the creation of this pattern that
supports me in holding it to me to affirm my worthlessness,
or my rage, or my entitlement to my anger.

"I choose today, once and for all, to decide I can change my
life for good. I affirm this now in the highest frequency available to me at my present state of awareness of my Christed
Self. I am Word through this intention. Word I am Word."

You have just created a basis for the clearing that you are
about to undertake. What we did was dismantle the initial
structure. In a way, we have replaced one thing with another.
We have replaced passivity with action and we have chosen
to create a way to clear what you need to clear in fullness and
in light.

We have to take a moment because Paul is shifting and his
system needs to ground for a moment so that we can continue with him. He has a boulder, too. He has several, and, of
course, as he was working with this exercise we were working
with him as well. He hears as he speaks, and the benefit of this
is that he can get the work done, too, and the downside is we
get to pause when we would like to talk.

But we are going to talk anyway. And we're going to talk
about the next step, and the next step of the clearing is to
actually create a frequency of a high enough level that you can

begin to clear the pattern in its cell memory of the body that you are in, which is also the attachment and the embellishment of it on many, many levels.

Now the cells of the body do have memory, and they can recall what they felt at any time in this life. And when those things are clearing that hold the memory, you can actually imprint them with new memory, new ideas, new ways of operating that do not embrace the old patterning. So what we would like to do now is bring light through you, through the center of your body, through the heart and the third eye, through the crown chakra, through the full light of your being to align you to the vibration of the Christ light.

"I am Word through my body. Word I am Word" aligns the body to the frequency of the Word. "I am Word through my vibration. Word I am Word" aligns the auric field and the frequency of the consciousness to the vibration of the Word. "I am Word through my knowing of myself as Word" replaces the lower self, the fear-based self, with the Higher Self, the Christed Self made into manifestation. "Word I am Word through this intention" anchors this. It affirms it and it seals it. "Word I am Word" is the punctuation. It's the ribbon on the package; it is the final seal, as it were.

What you do when you do this is you reclaim yourself on a fundamental level as your Christed Self. Now this Christed Self does not have a boulder in the living room. It can actually rise above it in consciousness, but ultimately those things that were created by you in fear, or in pain, or out of a need to defend must be cleared fully in order for you to progress in this practice of ascension. Your job today is to clear a boulder. And we are going to do it with you now.

What we first did was, we created the justification and the belief that this could be cleared and we let go of attachments to the boulder that may be unconscious or ways that we may use the boulder to protect us. For example, if I have a belief that I will not be loved, and that is the boulder in my room, I get benefits from that. I don't have to get too close to people, I can affirm my solitude, I can do lots of things, and it's a wonderful excuse. However, the dividend of pain that I am ultimately paying for that belief is large. So we will say yes, it is a creation and it is a boulder, so let's get rid of it.

The process of clearing a boulder is as follows:

"I am Word through this thing I see before me. Word I am Word. I am Word through this creation of pain that I have manifested for whatever reasons that is now obstructing my spiritual growth. I am now choosing to relinquish any and all attachments to this patterning of pain and all that it has created in my life. I am now willing to achieve a Christ consciousness that does not align to this pain but clears it from my cellular memory, from my auric field, from my awareness, from my physical reality in perfect ways.

"I am a Creator working in tandem with the Great Creator, I am a Light working with the Great Light, and I am a Christ working with the Great Christ in frequency. I am in alignment now with the vibration of the Word and I choose to release this boulder of pain in a perfect way that will result in my Creative Self working through this issue quickly, easily, and with consciousness. I am Word through this intention. Word I am Word."

"I am Word through this intention" states the intention that the Word is working through you to bring this into consciousness and then into manifestation in the physical realm. It sets in motion those events and those experiences that will be needed to support you in this clearing. It will not do the work for you, but it will embellish and set you on the path to work through this with frequency in perfect ways.

So we say to you today, if you have been a spinster longing for love and the love that you believe that you are not going to have has created a boulder for you, you will be set on a path and the boulder is being cleared in consciousness and in frequency from your cells, from your frequency, and from your consciousness. Once that is done, your physical reality will change and you will also be required to create a new thought to replace the old one.

So say, for example, you have always been frightened of

tigers and your fear of tigers is the boulder in your room, for lack of anything better. We would say to you that your knowing of your safety becomes the new thought. "I am in my safety with tigers" becomes the replacement thought. "I am in my companionship" replaces the thought of isolation. "I am in my perfect body and my perfect self" replaces the intentions or the beliefs to keep yourself in pain over your physical form or your health. Do you understand this?

Now we do this with you. So we said to you that you have set something in motion and I'm sure you would like to know what that process is. We say this. The process of experience for you will be one of saying, "I see it. I release it. I see it. I release it. I release it. I release it. It is gone."

But you will see it first. It will not vanish overnight. But when you see it, when you see the pattern in your face, when you have the experience, you Word through it. "I am Word through that I see before me" will bring this recognition of the pain, of the problem, of the issue before you into alignment into the Christ frequency, and that will support you in your healing of it. Period. It is done daily, it is an established exercise.

So if you want to know how you would clear an issue around compulsive eating, we will tell you this. You have already Worded through the issues and the creations and the attachment to the boulder itself. So now you have to deal with it on a level of consciousness, and when the issue rises and presents itself, you simply state, "I am Word through the need to engage in behavior that is not in support of my highest good. Word I am Word through this intention. Word I am Word." You clear the boulder before you with the creation of light.

Now we will tell you this. We do not guarantee you that you will complete this without your complete engagement to your identity as Word. When you can sort of say, "I am the Christed Self come into alignment with my own identity as Word," you can sort of get the benefits of it. Do you understand this? Now we are not telling you you have to stand on the mountain with wind blowing in your hair having the Ten Commandments under each arm and staring at a burning bush to know this. We are not telling you that at all. It is not that kind of experience. It's actually an experience of trust and belief in knowing that you are part of the Creator and that you are loved and that you are one with a higher frequency that is clearing you in the ways that are perfect for your growth.

Paul is wondering now, "Can anything be healed, really, or is that a joke? Are we misinforming people by saying that you can clear a boulder?" Why would we? is our answer to you. Why would we expend energy that takes time from you and from us to establish a false set of expectations? So that's the first answer. "Why would we tell you that" implies mistrust, and you are going to have to contend with that in whatever way is appropriate for you. The second thing we want to say is: Of course, anything can be healed. Anything can be changed. There are no miracles too small or too grand for the Creator. It is extended by you to the extent that your belief systems must respond in an elastic way to what you have required to come to you.

So say, for example, you are requiring a great deal of change at one time, but you do not believe that such a thing can be possible. Guess what? You are putting the brakes on and you are limiting the Creator and you are limiting the benefits that would otherwise be available to you in your consciousness. Do you understand this? This is what we did at the very beginning of the book when we talked about wonder. We actually told you very directly that in order for you to begin to express yourself in the consciousness of Word, you have to elasticize the belief system to embrace and experience wonder. Once you do that, you create room for possibilities. And once you do that, things change. We assure you, things change.

We do not take up the time of men and women for the sake of entertainment. We are past that. We are here to support you in achieving your goal, and this is a large mission on an individual level. And we also see that the benefits of this work have great implications for the consciousness of this planet. So we do the work with you for a selfish intention. We want to see the heralding of the Christ on this plane. We want to see the Christ risen in all men, and that is a frequency, it is a light, it is an awareness of his divinity on this plane incarnate. And we wish this for you in great love, great compassion, and the belief that this is so.

So we are gifting you today with a process that will support you in achieving this, because it's very hard to rise in frequency when you have a boulder hanging you down to the lower vibrations. So we are not just doing this for you to make you happy, although when you're happy, your frequency is much higher. We are doing this to establish you in a Christ frequency.

Now to the extent that you believe that the boulder will always be there, it will always be there. And we will say you are deeply loved anyway and you have not failed in any way. That is not what this is about at all. This is about creation, and what has been created will be uncreated if it is needing to create itself anew. If it does not happen today, it will happen. If it does not happen in this year, it will happen in another year or another lifetime, but ultimately your process of ascension is ongoing. We are giving you the fast track. All men are being fast-tracked. But we cannot take from you that which you believe you own and cannot release. And when we say you own it, you believe that it's yours and you will not release it.

When we speak of surrender, and we speak of surrender as, "God, I can't handle it, I can't take it, it is too big for me," what you are doing is you are releasing a boulder and you are aligning to the great powers that will clear it for you. We are doing the same thing with intention to the extent that you understand "I am Word" is not the ego self, it's not the personality. It is the Christ within you that achieves the work and deserves the glory. "I am Word through my problem" brings that action to the problem.

Now Paul is wondering, "Can't we just say, 'I give up'? Can't we just be powerless? It's so much easier than memorizing a meditation or standing on a corner and seeing everybody as perfect." We can say yes, if you want to surrender, you will be worked with at that level as well. There is beautiful integrity in surrender and miracles do happen. But if you can understand that one of the things that will happen, indeed, when you create a new pattern is that in likelihood you will be required to confront that thing that you have created and say, "I give up. I give it to the Christ. I am Word through this thing I see before me. Take it, take it, take it," you are also saying, "I am in the process of reclaiming myself as my Divine Self."

When the ego believes he can fix a broken leg, you have a doctor, perhaps, with a skill and some training who knows a system in the physical realm that can change and heal people. But the doctor itself does not heal the leg. The doctor can reset the bone; the body and the energy field of the body is in the process of healing itself. Period. Do you understand this?

When you say, "I am healing this man's wound in consciousness," your personality self is not healing that man's wound in consciousness. The healing is happening at a level of frequency. To the extent that you misalign your identity on a personality level with the healing frequency, you can make yourself fairly sick. Paul has had the experience as a healer of wanting somebody to be healed so badly that he depletes his own energy field, and in using his own energy field consciously to do the healing he was actually misappropriating his power. He was using his field as the source of the frequency as opposed to understanding that his energy field is the conduit.

Now we say to you this. The Creator works through you. To the extent that you self-identify with that frequency, you rise to it and your energy field can then work in tandem with it. "Of myself I am nothing, the Father within me doeth the work" is a way of stating this as well. The Christ within me, the God Self within me, the divinity that is within me, becomes me. I am self-identifying with that divinity, and to the extent that I have achieved this in a vibrational frequency I can begin to unfold my gifts in spirit, which means that I can be used on a higher level to support the healing and the transformation of others. But the moment I think it's me, the moment the person says, "I can fix you," you are dealing with an ego problem and a misalignment of energies.

We hope we have not complicated things for you. We are trying to keep this simple. But we want you to understand that your personality self is not taking an axe to a boulder. God within you is working on the boulder and the Word is the frequency of God in action. "I am Word through that which I see before me" creates anew that which is before me. "I am Word through this pain" clears the pain. "I am Word through my intention to release this pattern that creates this pain" sets that intention to release.

Paul sees in his mind's eye a rock clearing from his own third chakra, his own solar plexus attached to strings. And these are the attachments to the behavior. So when he says, "I am Word through the need to hold onto this pain," or "I am Word through the attachment or whatever holds this pain to me on any level," he can clear those things as well. You can be creative with your language, but please understand that language is a service. "In the beginning was the Word" is also saying, "Say it, say it, say it, say it." That's proof. "I am Word, I am Word, I am Word."

So now we tell you this. You have had a lesson today in clearing patterns of pain and we want to call this chapter "Boulders." And that's a silly name, but that has really been the focus of the chapter. And it will give you a memory and an image to work with when you see yourself suddenly facing things that you thought you would not have to look at because you have been avoiding them.

Paul is seeing a boulder in a living room with a woman walking around it with her dinner on a tray as if the boulder's not there. It's being ignored, but it takes up space. Now we want to see what happens when you state this intention:

"I am willing now to stand firm in my willingness to see that which I need to clear once and for all to bring me into alignment with my own Christed Self. I am willing to become aware of those behaviors and those patterns, those belief systems, those boulders of pain that stand in the way of my achievement and my design as a Christed Being come into form. I affirm now that I am being supported in this release in perfect ways by the energies, the powers, the guides, and the teachers who are working on this passage into Christed Self awareness and achievement. And I do this now with joy and with willingness. I am Word through this intention. Word I am Word."

What you have just done is set in motion the new willingness to change, to say, "Okay, I get it. I see it. I can deal with it, because I am not dealing with it now in the old way. I am dealing with it in the new way, which will align me to a higher frequency. And I am being shown the steps each step of the way to support myself in the clearings that are required to bring myself into achievement and alignment with the Christ consciousness. I am doing this now."

You have affirmed this. You have chosen it, and now get ready for it. You will see it, probably very quickly, and you have the tools now to begin to engage with it consciously, in an active way that will support you in the changes that you request.

Paul is asking now about unconscious behavior, and it is true that someone can be living in complete denial about a pattern of behavior that keeps her in isolation or in pain or in physical stress or in problem thinking or whatever. And it's perfectly appropriate to question whether or not these questions and problems will be addressed through the exercise of achievement we have gifted you with today. And the answer is yes. When someone is unconscious in a patterning, this will become presented to them in ways that they can handle. There will be a glimmer of recognition first, and an awareness of the pattern in a gentle way. And then, until the pattern is addressed and seen for what it truly is, it will make itself known in more significant ways. Do you understand this? So you all have opportunities.

So Paul is saying, "This means that we don't have to know what all our stuff is in order to go into the process?" And we say, of course. We do not expect you to know all your stuff. If you did, you probably wouldn't be reading this book. You would have found some other way to move forward in consciousness because you would have become very, very self-aware.

Now you are self-aware. We are not telling you anything other than you are choosing to engage now with these things that have created pain, that have kept you down, that have blocked you and kept you in a place of pain, fear, and anger. These things are boulders and you will and are dealing with them. Period.

Now we want to talk a bit about suffering and what suffering is. Suffering is a belief system that you attach to pain. You know this already: "Pain is pain, suffering is optional." It's a true statement. People suffer emotionally because it gives them what they need.

We will tell you this. Suffering is a creation and those who suffer actually are benefiting and gaining energy from what they are producing; otherwise it would not be so. But there are other reasons that suffering occurs that we wish to connect to and discuss.

(Pause)

Suffering is what occurs when man establishes a pattern of pain and then rotates it, as it were, through his consciousness and it cycles and cycles and cycles. Now sometimes when this happens, a creation is formed. A pain creation. And the pain creation hangs out in the auric field and feeds off the energy of what is being expressed emotionally, and we can call this if you wish, a parasitic energy or a demon, although we dislike the word because it has connotations to it that are inappropriate, misleading, and create fear. This is not a chapter on demons. This is a discussion of boulders.

We're going to talk about these energies of suffering as creations that can be cleared through intention. So say you have a pattern of suffering that is in place, and we are speaking of emotional suffering: "I am so beleaguered. I am so in my suffering." Well, that can be vanity, but we are speaking of something where someone is truly suffering emotionally and can't seem to stop herself either from her obsessive thinking or her brutality to her emotional self. We want to clear these things, too, and we want to do this in a different way.

We actually want to bring the light of Christ to the belief that the suffering is required. That is the first thing. The belief that the suffering is required actually holds the suffering in place, and the attachment to suffering, the attachment to living in the problem all the time must be cleared as well, as we did earlier, so that any emotional attachments that one has to it can be cleared and released.

And now we want to talk about what it means to clear an energy frequency that you have created in worry or in fear that has taken on its own little self-hood and hangs out and causes trouble. We want to address this, and we are pulling Paul back because this kind of discussion gives him reason for pause. But we want to say this. We are not talking about exorcisms, we are not talking about anything other than clearing patterns of creation that have been set in motion by you, in response to circumstance, that have their own energy frequency and agenda.

If you can imagine that every time you say the word "Nebraska," a light lights up in your energy frequency and goes, "Ding ding ding, it's time for the Nebraska tape to play," you will understand what we are talking about. But in this case, it's not the word "Nebraska." It's usually something that triggers a pattern, or creates a pattern that's already been established if someone is in a constant state of suffering. So we say to you this. How you clear this stuff is through the intention to align your frequency to the Christ vibration. And you will do this as follows:

"I am Word through my intention to now release myself from any energies that are externalized or have been created by me that operate independently from my own consciousness, that may be impacting me in a negative way. I am now choosing to release any and all parasitic energies that I may be holding in my frequency that are not mine, that are inherited culturally or have been given to me or created by me in any lifetime for any reason. I am now resolved that I am being supported in this release by my guides and teachers, and that I am cleared perfectly of any negativity that has created suffering and the pattern of suffering in my life. I am Word through this intention. Word I am Word."

We're going to address Paul's concerns right now, because he's sitting there on a stool, thinking, "Aha! What's this about?" This is simply about another way of clearing energy. And once again, you have attachments to language so that when you say "parasitic energy," you move into another kind of vocabulary that you are not comfortable with.

We are only saying that man can create a frequency that operates independently from him. And this is usually done through a repetitive thought or through serious trauma that creates a belief system, or through suffering when suffering is not done intentionally, as a way of keeping the self in pain for conscious reasons. And these reasons can include all of the benefits one gets from being the one who suffers. But when suffering is not created for those reasons, it must be contended with somehow. And real suffering is rarely a condition that is established casually. So we don't want to address it casually.

Now Paul is saying, "Why do I see this as my mind's eye as something that is in the auric field? Like a ball, or an emblem, or a figure?" Well, we say these are ways that you can identify these things in order to make them real enough for you in order to clear them. You all have attachments and cords to those patternings and behaviors and energies in your life. And the clearing of these things is actually part of what we are engaging with. So this is just part of a process.

Paul earlier saw a boulder in a living room. And we will say this. That was the appropriate image for that clearing. A little ball hanging out and causing trouble in the auric field is appropriate for this one as well. We hope that this has made sense to you.

Now we want to give you an exercise to carry you through to the next time you meet, and we encourage you to do this on your own today or tonight before you sleep.

We want you to see yourself standing before yourself as perfect. As a perfect creation with no embellishments. We ask you to see yourself idealized. Your perfect body. Your perfect physical health. Your perfect emotional state. The perfect smile on your face. The being that you truly are in perfection as realized before you. We want you to spend time observing this person. We want you to imprint this image of this perfect person in your consciousness. We want you to experience them first tonight as something that you see outside of yourself from every angle. See yourself before you, naked in your perfection, glowing, beautiful in your wonder, in your wisdom, as the perfect creation that you are intended to be.

We will come back to this image tomorrow and we will begin to work with it in a much more direct fashion. You are seeing yourself as you truly are, and we are going to honor this through the exercises that are to come. We give you praise for your willingness to engage with this text, with these words, and with the energies that work with us to bring you into consciousness.

Word I am Word. Thank you and goodnight.

SIX

IDENTIFYING AS WORD

March 8, 2009

Okay, we're going to talk now. And we left you yesterday standing before a mirror in which you envisioned yourself in your perfection. And you saw yourself as you truly are, without blemish, without fear, without any distortion, because you saw yourself in your perfection. And what this actually means is that your perfect self is the perfectly created self, made by the spiritual self that manifests into form.

Now you may not like what you see when you look in a little mirror, but when you look in the big mirror, in the cosmic mirror as it were, what you are reflecting back to you is the image and likeness of God. And we say "perfection" is not a wrong word to use when you want to understand that you are an aspect of the Creator in form. So yes, we are saying to you that you are perfect, inherently perfect, manifested in perfection, and that is your true state of being.

We are speaking now on an energetic level. We are not

talking about the pimple on your nose, or the saddlebags, or the misformed appendage that you may have. We are not discussing that. We are discussing your True Self in manifestation as energy as manifested as the Christ.

Now please understand this. When something is manifested in spirit that has to manifest in physical form as well. We are not telling you at this moment that you have a perfect self hanging out in a cosmic mirror that isn't real and you cannot access. We are telling you that you are this perfect being and you might as well start understanding that now so you can get about the business of becoming this in the physical form that you stand in.

Now this means you can be healed and you can be changed. It does not mean that we can undo things, in some cases, that have been presented to you karmically or through physical changes that cannot be rebirthed in this body. We are going to give you an example. On an etheric level, in your spiritual body you have all four limbs, all of your organs are in place. On the physical level, you may have had something taken out or something removed. On the spiritual level, your body remains perfect. Yes, Paul, that is why people have phantom pains after an amputation. The limb on the etheric is still experiencing itself as whole and the body remembers it. On a cellular memory, you actually hold the memory of every trauma that has ever been induced to your physical self. So falling off the bicycle that we told you about chapters before is actually retained in the cellular memory of the body, as is the scalpel, as is the scrape, as is the memory of any pain the physical body has endured.

In a perfect state, the etheric body is magnificent and still whole. As we are clearing the memory of trauma from the physical self, we are also bringing in the light to clear the memory and repattern it in the vibration of the Word. When I say, "I am Word through my limb," I am affirming my limb is in its perfection, and if the physical limb is no longer there to be perfect, it is still perfect on the spiritual planes.

You can't imagine in any image you might have of heaven that you walk around with that bad foot. You know perfectly well that on a spiritual level you are healed in that manifestation. In your imagination even, you can't imagine that that backache would still hurt you in an idealized heaven. And that's because there's already an aspect of yourself that understands that the physical form is a temporary inhabitation of this soul that you exist in lifetime after lifetime. And that soul, my friends, is a perfect creation at a higher level that is coming into itself as the Christ consciousness through a series of teachings, lifetimes, experiences, and is now fast-tracking itself through the reading of this book and the application of the information therein.

So on a cellular level, the body can retain the memory of pain. On an emotional level, the body can retain the imprinting of pain, which is why, of course, you jerk back in anticipation of pain when you think of something painful. You wouldn't touch something that you knew was hot. You would draw your finger back because you know, from experience, what it feels like to be burned. So on a very practical level, cell memory has a purpose. We don't want you to forget that it hurts to put your hand in a fire. That would not serve anybody. So you know what you need to know. We are discussing, though, when a distortion occurs, when a pain pattern is created that makes you feel reflected in a distorted way.

If you have an idealized self that you can begin to imagine and work with, the self that we spoke of yesterday in our teaching, the one who stands before you naked and perfect, that will be the way in for you today. Because really, what we are going to do today is disguise that self in such a way that you can actually believe that that is who you are.

Now Paul is already going, "I must have misheard. Disguise? You just told us to see ourselves as perfect."

Disguise is actually correct, because on a certain level it would feel like a joke to you to merge with your perfect body, with your true self, and say, "Okay, I guess I lost thirty pounds. I guess my hair grew back. I guess that blemish that's been making me crazy is not there anymore," and you throw the book across the room. That's why we're saying we're disguising you. And we're disguising you on a higher level so that you can actually reemerge as this self through this process.

We are taking you through a process now of decision making. And here is decision one:

> "Am I entitled to be in my perfect self, in a perfect manifestation of myself that translates into physical form? Am I now allowing myself to have permission to believe that this can be so?"

If you answer, "Yes," make a mental check. That is the first requirement. If you already believe on your heart level that this cannot be so, this will not happen. If your consciousness or if your self, in a smaller way, can begin to give permission to the possibility that this is truthful, we will take you through this process and you will undergo it. So you have made decision one, yes or no. If you have said, "No," put the book down and take a walk and then come back with a new decision, because we'll work with you then just as readily. This is really in your time.

The body knows already that it is made in the image and likeness of God. That is in the DNA of the body. The body knows that it is a vehicle for the spirit. The ego self, the false self, is the one that decides what can happen when in this regard. And it will actually tell the body, "You're fat and old," or "You don't need this," or "It can't happen anyway," and then the body goes back and says, "Okay." But on a true level, the body is in understanding already that it can be transformed. It needs to be repatterned, it needs to be accepted, and it needs to be allowed to come into its form at a higher frequency.

Once you have a higher frequency that vibrates through the physical form, the physical form begins to change to appropriate the mold that is created on the etheric level, and that is a perfect form. Do you understand this? So once you say, "I am willing to believe I can inhabit this form," you can begin to change it. You decide. We have said this many times. You decide that you can be in the form as much as you decide that you can have what you want in a higher frequency and conform to the belief that this is so. So that was decision one.

Decision two is a different kind of decision. It's a decision about the willingness to acquire the ability to emerge from this process with new abilities that you will hold in consciousness that will then be translated into your experience in the physical realm.

Now Paul, right now, is a man in his forties who is sitting in a chair with a dog beside him in a body that could use a lot of work and still we are able, somehow, to transmit through him a book in regards to the creation of the Christed Self manifesting in man. He is not that special in this regard. He can be this man and transcribe something very differently, but the book that is coming through him right now is about the manifestation of perfection, of the Christed Self becoming himself in man. He has an ability to hear.

Now get this, everybody. You all have the ability to become a tuning fork for the higher frequencies. You are intended to be this. So now we ask you to decide if you are willing to claim your abilities at a higher frequency that will amount to a complete transformation of how you understand your perspective in the physical realm.

We say to you this. When we started with Paul some years ago, we had to give him experience that was physical because he didn't believe in anything much, and he was desirous of believing but he was terrified of misunderstanding or misbelieving or doing it wrong. So we actually had to come up with ways to break through his resistance to understand that the physical realm was only an aspect of reality. He was given an experience very early that woke him up and as a result he began to see lights floating around people in their energy field. This was proof enough to him that there was something happening and he could be able to trust what he could see, so that engaged him on a journey.

Right now, when you work with your own consciousness, you are doing so within the parameters and structures that you have believed you had access to as a soul, as a personality, as a body. You have these ideas of what can and cannot transpire. Paul did as well, everybody does, and they are all very different. So we say to you, the benefits that we can give you by transforming your experience on a physical level, which include the development of your higher capacities to experience energy as sight, as feeling, or as hearing (and we will use the words for you if you wish—*clairvoyance, clairaudience, clairsentience*—which means to feel frequency, to feel spirit in energy), if we have these things available to you, we simply ask right now that you ask yourself if you believe that you can begin to develop them as God-given abilities and not something that is in the province of the lunatics or the mystics, whatever your belief system is.

You have to say on a certain level that "I will allow myself to begin to experience my experience in a dimensional way that exceeds the limitations that I was told I was allowed to have." When you say, "Yes," to this, you actually unlock a door in perception, in the perception of other realms of experience. And they can begin to address you through your consciousness.

We spoke a few minutes ago about your being a tuning fork to the higher vibrations. That is one aspect of this work. You already are this. Everybody is. But it's the refinement of the ability that allows you to have the level of experience that will transform your consciousness in an experiential way about the planet and the vibration that you exist in.

Let us give you an example. If you are a schoolteacher and one day the energy fields of all your students start to glow, you may fall over because you haven't seen it before. But really all that's happening is your dimensional ability is transforming. Your third eye, which is the sixth chakra, which is the energy system that allows you to see into the higher realms, is activated and clear and you have lifted your frequency to the level where this is possible for you. Then you have a practical experience of vibrational energy and the benefits that come as you develop as a conscious being. Now you can see things. So what does it mean? It means that you can begin to access information through your energy field and frequency that will help other people. Period. This is not selfish. To be able to see somebody's frequency or be able to hear somebody tele-pathically, which is what Paul is doing now, these are abilities that you are intended to have for the purpose of refinement and growth, and part of growth is to be in service to your fellow man.

If Paul sees a client and predicts the stock market, he is actually doing practical work. But we hope that the client is supported in this work in such a way that he will begin to believe that he has the ability himself to manifest this gift. Guess what, everybody? You cannot manifest these gifts without going through a process of acclimation to a spiritual frequency that will support you in your changes. We are not opening up a psychic school. This is not about psych-ism or responding to matter in selfish ways. This is simply about showing you that who you are on a perfect level has intended abilities that have not come into manifestation because you have been told by society, by yourself, or by other people that you cannot do it. You have been lied to. You have been lied to. You have been lied to.

Now some of this lie is actually about control. When man begins to move out of the matrix of believing that he is sub-jugated by a religion or by rules that are about controlling the mind through belief systems that keep man small and disempowered—and that is a matrix that we will tell you that we are dismantling now at a consciousness level on a grand scale to achieve this goal—when man realizes that he is free to believe what he wants to believe and what he can believe, he will make a shift in consciousness so that miracles, what you perceive to be miracles, can happen readily.

To see the soul of another man is a huge gift. To look into the eyes of a woman and see the perfection that she truly is is a magnificent moment. To lay the hands on a child in the knowing that child can be healed is a deep privilege in service to your Creator. We do not do this from a place of ego. We do this from a place of liberation of consciousness. And part of the liberation of consciousness is, of course, to realize how completely interconnected you all are as energy frequencies. You are a huge group of energy configurations tied together, bumping into one another in your perfection all the time. The illusion in the separateness of your Creator has manifested finally in the belief that you are separate from one another. And the first step towards realizing your unity with your Cre-ator is to understand that all men are one.

"Our Father" is the beginning of the Lord's Prayer. "Our Father." Think of this. We are all one connection, born of the same frequency, born of the same energy that we can define or name as the Universe, God, the Creator, what have you. "Our Father" signifies this truth. Every religion will have this imprinted in its doctrine because it is a fact. It does not belong to Christianity any more than it belongs to the pagan beliefs of the Goddess. Everybody believes that there is One Source, ultimately, at the highest level.

Now we will not go into history and the beliefs in multiple Godheads for this treatise, only to say that above that level of multiple Gods there was always a Great Creator pulling the strings. You can actually decide that God can be manifested in multiple ways and create a system of theology that will work very well. And we tell you that the belief in the Father and the Son and the Holy Spirit is an example of this. But what that is really doing is codifying energetic frequencies and alignments and relationships to try to understand and differentiate the action of the spirit as it expressed in man and in universal truth. That is what that is.

But what we were telling you is, "Our Father" signifies the unity of all men and to understand yourself as one with the Father, that requires you to become inclusive of your fellows, like it or not. The one that you can't stand is still your brother, like it or not. Period. End of sentence.

Going back for a moment to the treatise on perfection that we began with: If you are perfect in a higher frequency and you can begin to accept this and make the decision, "Yes, I can accept this," and then the second decision, "Yes, I am willing to believe that I can incorporate and inhabit the gifts of the spirit through my consciousness to develop the abilities of responding, and seeing and feeling frequency at a higher level," then you will say, "I am ready for this."

We are not making you supermen. We do not ascribe to that belief. We are saying you are already, you just forgot it. You forgot it. You forgot it. Period.

So the next step for you as a culture is to begin to respond to yourselves as Divine Beings. If everybody does this in a certain way, everybody is transformed. How this begins is through you and your fellow and the person sitting next to you. And guess what, everybody? You can support the transformation of your fellow through your own perfection. We said before, this is not about selfishness. Once you begin to vibrate at a higher frequency, your energy field vibrates in such a way that it impacts matter. And when you impact matter, you experience it in your own field.

We want to speak for a moment about empathy and the different ways that empathy can manifest. Paul serves as an empath. That is his work. He can sit before somebody and ask to "feel" them, and he will feel in his body, or what he believes to be his body, where injury has occurred, and then he can bring information forth about the injury or perhaps support it in healing. He can hear what people say on a telepathic level and feel what they feel. Again, he is not special. He has simply refined his energy systems to the ability to tune into others, and when he works with someone else on a practical level he forgets that he is separate long enough to experience them through his own energy systems. He does not have a broken leg, but he feels the broken leg for a moment of the person opposite him who had that injury several years before. That's what we are saying.

Now this applies to you on a practical level. By giving you this example, we are giving you permission to begin to have this experience yourself. And you haven't had this experience, for the most part, because you didn't believe you were allowed to, or that it was humanly possible.

Now you don't need to become a healer in order to benefit from knowing what somebody else feels, or to operate at a higher level of listening. So you can begin to know yourself or communicate with the higher frequencies in ways that are appropriate to you. This can happen for you and you can be worked with to develop these skills, and we will call them skills—not gifts, skills—in ways that are appropriate to you.

So right now we wish to do an exercise.

Imagine right now that you are imagining someone you know and that you care for. But you do this neutrally. "I see before me the image of my uncle Frank, or my friend Joey, or the woman I know at work that I like, Joan." And you see them, and you name them, before you, in your mind's eye. Now we would like you to do this. We want you to imagine for a moment that you know, and we underline the word *know*, what they feel like, and then you begin to experience that feeling in your own energy system.

You have to ask yourself now, "What did it feel like to be Joan, or Joey, or Frank? What impressions did I get? Did I feel thirsty? Did I want a cigarette? Did my back hurt? Were my eyes tired? Did I suddenly feel like I had a headache, or I was getting angry for no apparent reason?" When you do this, you are beginning to access information on a level of consciousness through frequency.

Now we are not doing this in any way that is invasive or in violation of the energy systems of those you tune in to. This is always done with permission on a higher level. Paul sometimes tunes in to people who say, "No," and he says, "Okay," and that's perfectly appropriate, at times, to "no." That's what we will say.

(Pause)

To develop the ability of sentience, clairsentience, clear feeling, is what you will do when you begin to move through your energy frequencies and understand that they are connected to the person next to you, and the person next to you, and the person next to you. And this awareness will benefit you in remarkable ways, because what it has to do, what it cannot help doing, is decide for you that you are interconnected to your fellows. You cannot do this and believe for a moment that you are separate.

We will discuss hearing now and what this means, and the ability to hear. We are not speaking to Paul as if he is on a telephone. His physical ears are actually not even involved in this process. The thought is imprinted into him, and because he trusts our energies, he aligns to this and he is able to hear and repeat. It's as if the word is imprinted in his mind. He hears it in his frequency and he can work with it then. It's not that different when you are walking around the street and suddenly a thought occurs to you that blocks out all the other thoughts and then you begin to respond to it, if you understand what we mean.

What we are actually telling you is that frequency can be translated into thought that can be "heard," for lack of a better word, and that is your own guidance. Now we recommend first and foremost that you decide right now that you can hear yourself at a higher level. That you can hear your True Self. And this is important.

Right now you're in a habit, more than likely, of listening to your fear, to the fear-based self, or the self that is dismissive or says it can't be done. But you can tell yourself now that you have permission to know yourself and to know your thoughts at the higher frequency. Because they are your thoughts, they will respond to you. You are not asking to hear Methuselah or your dead aunt Jenny. You are simply asking to hear your own knowing in your consciousness in a way that you can respond to.

A practice of meditation will support this greatly and we recommend it highly to the serious student of study of spiritual growth. But at this moment we want to say even the girl who has no time to meditate has the right and the privilege of hearing herself and knowing her own mind.

So at this moment in time we say to you:

"I am now choosing to hear myself, to know myself, to communicate with myself in the higher frequencies. I know what I know and the fear-based voice is being replaced once and for all by the Higher Self, the Christed Self that knows who he is. I am Word through this intention. Word I am Word."

Now you have set this intention. You will set it again when you forget it again. "I am hearing my Higher Self. Word I am Word through this intention. Word I am Word." This will support you.

And in our case right now, we are using the term "Higher Self" to signify that aspect of the self that is already knowing, that is already in formation, and has the answers you require. So we recommend this: that when you meditate, or when you decide you can sit with yourself for any length of time, you decide as an exercise that you will tune in as if you are a radio to your own higher knowing and then see what happens.

It really is about attunement, you know, and nothing more than that. It's as if you are a radio and the frequencies are bombarding you all the time but the radio doesn't play all the frequencies, it chooses the frequencies it hears. And you can decide now that you are aligned to a higher frequency and that is what your radio is playing.

Spirit guides. We gave this thought to Paul right now because it's the next question that we will address. "How do I hear my spirit guides? Do I have them?"

Yes, of course you do, and you already hear them. And you hear them in different ways depending on how you operate and what stage of development you are at. Some people actually see them. They sit in the car and have a conversation with them. Paul does not do this. He thinks if he did, he would lock himself up. Even he has limitations still about what he believes is appropriate or what he is allowed to do and we are working on that with him as part of the process of this book. Because to the extent that anyone keeps himself in limitation, he keeps himself in the denial of spiritual growth. Do you understand this?

Now some people can see them, some people can hear them, some people can feel them, some people can know them, but most of you, actually, just understand on a higher level that you are supported in spirit. It is very important for someone who is new on this path to get the concept that there are those beings on another dimensional level who are in support of their growth.

You've heard the saying, "When the student is ready, the teacher appears," and this is deeply true. For any student of spiritual growth who requires growth and states the intention to grow in some humility will be brought to a teacher who will work with them. And we say humility by saying, throwing a temper tantrum and saying, "Why aren't I in audience with the Dalai Lama yet?" isn't going to get you anywhere. And it's not a very evolved way of approaching the question. But if you say, "I am willing to grow and I am affirming that I am being directed in spirit to those teachers and to that information that would support me," in fact, it is guaranteed to happen. Then you have to use your discernment about what is appropriate for your growth, because not all teachers are appropriate for all students, nor are all teachers telling the truth, and we say that with sadness.

Many people who have an investment in control become teachers. And there are wonderful teachers in any school and then there are the ones that are not so good. Your own experience as a student will show you this. And we recommend this: that when you study with a teacher, you learn from someone who is also engaged in his or her own learning and moving through their own issues, because then you can be in service as they are in service. You choose people who acclimate to the vibration that you feel most comfortable with, and that is affirming to you. Not all teachers are appropriate to all students at the given time that they are approached. They may be later, they may never be, but you must be in your discernment. Period.

Now going back to your spirit guides. Everybody has memory of being led at some time or another in their lives. You are walking to the store, and then you had a strange urge to walk in another direction, and then you bumped into someone you needed to know. You were having a "feeling" about something and then you responded to the feeling, or you didn't respond and you discounted the feeling, only to learn later that had you responded, something wonderful might have occurred. Your guides are always working with you to support you in your growth. That is their investment in you. And they are growing and learning through these interactions as well. Everybody is evolving. It is not a static thing. We evolve, the spirits, the teachers, the guides, the energies that are teaching through this book, are evolving as well. Everything changes and moves forward, and your guides teach you in their ability as they grow with you.

So if you want to understand that your guides have an investment in your growth because they also benefit, you might stop looking at them as a taskmaster or as a beneficial angel like Tinker Bell that floats around you but you can't really have a relationship with.

Now we say to you this. You are already in relationship
with your guides. You already are. On a higher level you talk,
you know each other, and you meet, in some strange space.
Paul is surprised at this statement because that has not been
his experience of growth in this regard, but it is very true.
Everybody is already in communication at a higher frequency,
they just don't always know it. Yes, your dream states are ways
that you access your guides and the teachings available to you,
but that's only one way. On other dimensions there's a great
deal of dialogue going on with you about your requirements
for your own growth.

So we say to you this. To begin to trust that you have a
spirit guide or an angel or a guardian or a personal teacher
is to your benefit, because then you will believe that you are
being supported in this passage. As you believe, you increase
your frequency and you align to your own higher frequency in
such a way that will make the meeting with your own guides
possible. Yes, Paul, this will be addressed again in a later chapter of this book.

For this moment in time we want to return to our ini-
tial statement, which had to do with your perfection. We
keep digressing and coming back with an intention that
each time we come back to the ideal of perfection and your
own perfection, you are becoming more comfortable with
it. That your idealized self, which has been hanging out

now for several pages waiting patiently for your recognition, will become more familiar to you with each pass of the mirror.

We say to you now: We want to do an exercise for you that will embrace you with your own Higher Self, your own Christed Self, the manifestation of the perfect self that we have discussed. And we want to take you through this in a way…[pause]…We were saying in your magnificence, you stand before yourself, and we will take you now through this exercise of choice and responsibility. To say "choice" means that you choose it. To say "responsibility" means that you have the requirements to continue on this path by saying, "Yes." When you say, "Yes," you are in choice; when you are in responsibility, you are in the requirements of forward motion.

Your idealized self is the out-picturing of who you truly are. Not as you wish to be, but who you truly are on a Christed level. If you are a small woman and you wish to be taller, you can imagine that, but we're not going to lengthen your bones, or increase your bust, or change your eye color. That is not what we mean by your idealized self. Your idealized self is the perfect creation of God in form. Period. Your self in your perfected state. The manifestation of this and the merging with this is the exercise that we intend to undertake with you in frequency now.

You stand before yourself perfectly in your requirements for your own growth. And you believe that this self that we told you would be disguised is going to merge with you. Now we will go back to the ideal for a moment. When you stand before yourself in your perfected state, you stand before the mirror that is your true consciousness. You are in your consciousness and you are regarding yourself perfectly as the perfect creation you truly are. We witness you as this. We decide with you, "Yes, yes, yes, this can be so."

So in this moment in time we set this intention: "I am Word through my intention to merge once and for all with my truly created self that is in perfection before me. I am Word through this intention. Word I am Word."

Now we ask your energy field to begin to merge with that perfect being that we see before you. We ask your self to believe that this being is connecting to you and becoming you and imprinting you with its requirements for transformation.

Now we want to talk about a disguise and what we actually meant by that. We did not mean a funny nose or a fright wig on your Higher Self. We simply want you to understand that the magnificence of what you are is in deep contrast to how you perceive yourself. So if you see yourself in an idealized state, you are actually working with yourself in an uncorrupted form that we can work with to manifest into you. However, if you were to see yourself as your Christed Self in truth, the light would stagger you and you would back away from this promise because the implications would be too large for your conscious mind to appreciate fully. You would say, "It can't be done."

It is being done. This is not a self-help book. Understand this. We have an investment in you feeling better because it raises your frequency and it reminds you on a higher level that you are entitled to it, and that's important. But this is not a diet book. It's not about feeling better about yourself as you make hard decisions. It's not one of these books at all. It is a primer of the manifestation of the Christed Self in man. Get it? That's what we are doing. And isn't that outrageous? We think so. We know you do. And yet still, we take the time to sit here and disseminate this information in order to bring forth this action. The merging with the self that we are undertaking now is a requirement for this to occur. And we are going to do it again, but differently.

"I see before me a bridge. And this bridge leads me to this next stage of my evolution as a conscious being. On this bridge I see before me my perfected self. My perfected self reaches a hand out and guides me across this bridge one step at a time, affirming that we are one energy and we can be merged in a perfect way.

"As I step off the other side of my bridge, I see before me my Perfected Self in all its glory. A manifested being of high consciousness and perfect light. And my arms open to embrace this beautiful being that I now know to be myself in truth. And I merge completely with my Higher Self, with the Christed frequency that I truly am in spirit. I become one with the Christ in myself, as myself, with myself, and through myself.

"I am Word through this intention to merge completely with my Christed Self. Word I am Word."

We ask you now. We ask you now, do you want to know something about what this really means? This means that your life is changed. It is changed. It is changed.

What we have done with you now on a level of frequency is transform your energy field into a recognition of himself, herself as who he and she is in consciousness. And as the Christ in consciousness, you begin to believe yourself as truthfully vibrating in the frequency of Word.

Now this is not a momentary occurrence. You do not go to the grocery store and say to the checkout clerk, "Hi, I'm Word, I'd like to use my credit card today." You don't do that. That would be ridiculous. But we say that the imprinting that is occurring in you right now will manifest in frequency and consciously in your consciousness as you transform the obstacles that have been created to this occurrence. Again, you have made a choice to merge with your own energy as the Christed Self. And this is a miracle.

Paul is saying, "But that was a short meditation. How did we manage that?" It is managed at a level of consciousness. On a level of individual consciousness through the assent and confirmation of a soul who says, "I am willing to merge with my own Christed Self and realize myself as Word." When this is done, it can happen, it will happen, and there is nothing that can stop it. It is made so.

Paul requests an explanation. "What does it mean, 'It can't be stopped'?" What it means is that you have set in motion a change in your being and in your frequency. You have bought the ticket for the ride, you have been on the ride, and now you have said, "I am staying on the ride, I am going to see this through," and the current is going.

We said earlier in this text that when a seed is planted, the obligation of the seed is to realize itself as what it is intended to be. And the manifestation of the Christ is no different. The Christ that is within you, "Word I am Word" if you wish, the manifestation of this is coming into being. How long it will take is up to you, because you have requirements for your growth. You each do. And this does not absolve you of any responsibility. In fact, it requires you to face yourself again and again and again and regard yourself as perfect, and a perfect creation of the Father, of the Universe, of the Christed Self made manifest. Because that will then enable you to transform, to release, to transmute those energies that impede this being from coming into being in its completeness.

Yes, Paul. Paul is seeing an image right now of a clay mask placed over his face. And this mask looks like an old Greek mask, a terra cotta mask of a man with a beard. And this mask is beginning to crack open. It's beginning to splinter. And as it does so, a great light is beginning to work through it. To manifest the self as the Christed Self requires this mask that each of you wears, this false self that has said to you, "I cannot be myself as my Christed Self," to fall apart and dismantle once and for all.

Paul, for the first time, just saw himself as beginning this experience, and it was shown to him for the reason that we could tell you what it meant. Now very simply, when you move through this process, you have to understand that you are being escorted by the text on two different levels. On the level of instruction, which is the words on the page, and the level of frequency, which is sponsorship. You are being sponsored frequency-wise in your own dismantling of the false self, of the big clay mask, of the safety of the ego that wants to release now because it can now transform into something greater.

So we say to you this. Your choice now is to regard the self as perfect. As this perfect creation you have aligned to. And we will give you an exercise that you will take out into the world today to work with consciously.

"I am now standing on a street corner, and my own perfection is reflected back to me through all that I see. I am experiencing myself as my Perfected Self in consciousness. And what is reflected back at me is my own perfection. I have wisdom now available to me and I will ask myself what I need to know. I have understanding available to me and I will consciously connect to my understanding in a way that will give me the information and knowing that I require. I listen with new ears, as I understand the requirements for my own growth. I am Word through this intention, to know myself, to experience myself, as my Christed Self. Word I am Word through this intention. Word I am Word."

Paul is requesting that we speak more about the empathic gifts or abilities that we spoke of earlier. We will tell you only this. As you continue to regard the self as perfect, and as you can understand the perfection in your fellows, this will begin to happen naturally. It is a benefit. To be able to feel what people are feeling only serves you if you are in spirit and regarding them as spirit. It's not a tool to get what you want. It means you understand, you can serve, and you can know. So while we will discuss things like this in subsequent chapters, we have put a close on that one for now.

In leaving you today, we want to discuss one thing more, and that is choice as it relates to discussion with others about this work that you are doing now. You must believe in your own way that you are choosing this and this is not being foisted on you or responded to in a way that is to your—

P. Other word. Other word. Other word, I'm not hearing.
Other word.

—The response that is negative. You are not hearing right, Paul, because you are blocking. So we are going to start this thought again.

When you discuss this journey with others, you must maintain your resolve to be in your higher truth. You must decide today that the way you will talk about this experience will not be used by you in a way to disregard it, to diminish your experiences with it thus far, or to foist it on another as a requirement for their own growth. Those who require this text will be brought to it. You can believe this. Those who require this text for their own growth and benefit will be taught by us in the way that is most appropriate for them. There will be other ways and other texts to follow. Some will be through us, but many, many, many right now are receiving this information in different cultures and different ways and setting in motion the creation of Word made manifest.

So we say to you this. When you have an opportunity to discuss this, know that you must stay in the frequency of the book. It's not a lot different than if you go on a date with someone and then you get very excited and then you tell your friend Nancy and she says, "Oh, that guy, you don't wanna talk to him," and then your energy and enthusiasm diminish.

You simply have to decide now that you can have this text in your experience and support yourself if you share your choices with your fellows, and you will, and we support you in this beneficially and with pleasure. We give you praise now for your industry and for your commitment to standing firm in your own vibration.

> "I am Word through my being. Word I am Word. I am Word through my consciousness. Word I am Word. I am Word through that which I perceive, that which I hear, that which I know, and that which I understand. I am Word. I am Word. I am Word. So be it."

Thank you and goodnight.

SEVEN

NAVIGATION

March 9, 2009

We're going to talk about life today, and the requirements of life once you have transformed yourself into the Higher Self that you are choosing to make manifest through this process of undertaking this book.

You are capable of great change. Every man, every woman is capable of great change. Now change, in its current form, to you implies doing something different, being someplace different, acclimating in a different way to different things. This is true. This is appropriate. And in many ways the changes that you will be undertaking are those kinds of changes. But the deep change, the larger change, the change that is truly promised, is a change in consciousness. It's a change in how you experience yourself on a moment-to-moment level, as you exist in this physical body.

Up until now the higher frequencies, which have always

been present, have been aligned in such a way that it took a great deal of time to move upwards to exist in the higher realms. Throughout time there have been people on a chosen path, as it were, who have decided and aligned to their progress as their priority and their incarnations over time prepared them for the alignment that they eventually received. And these are the people you think of who have manifested great gifts, not necessarily psychic gifts, but gifts of the spirit, who have changed things, who have made manifest changes in this world through their consciousness.

Now in these days the planetary grid, the place that you live in, is actually changing. The planet that you exist in is actually heightening its frequency. Or we would better say, those who exist on this planet, every living thing, is frequency and this frequency of every living thing is changing. And as the physical people, every living thing, on this planet transforms itself through integrating the higher frequencies that are currently available to them, everything has to change. So we speak right now of mass change. Not just the change in the individual who wants a higher experience of frequency, but the impact of this on a larger level is deeply, deeply significant.

When a group of people decide that they can have a different existence, they begin to inform things. This country actually was built on that principle, and this country has operated on those principles to one degree or another for some time.

When a world decides in consciousness, in agreement, that it can go up a level in vibration—up a level means to a higher consciousness—the whole planet must change to accommodate this shift, because as you know, thought creates, impacts, and finalizes the physical realm. You cannot make something without thinking about it first, and when everybody is thinking the same thought, matter changes. Period.

You will begin to have experiences of this as a planet in the coming years because the trials that are present currently are really about transformation. And as this transformation is undertaken, the benefits of it will begin to be seen. But just as we said, the experience of the individual is only part and parcel of this response to the individual changes in frequency. The larger changes that impact everybody are also in motion. So that is the way things are unfolding.

Now once you understand that your choice right now is to embark on this consciousness shift with a decision, your life actually gets easier. Everybody is going through this shift. We can tell you that. When we said fast track, we didn't mean fast track only for those of you who were special enough, privileged enough, thoughtful enough to decide to buy this book. Wouldn't that be ridiculous, to have consciousness available only to the few of you who put down the money and sat on a bench and did this reading? That would actually be antithetical to this purpose.

We say to you this. Everybody is undergoing this transformation in consciousness. Those of you who've picked up the book have tools and a vocabulary with which to understand these changes. That's the difference. This is not a how-to book in how to get awakened over a series of days. The benefit of this book is to become awakened through your own focus and alignment with the higher frequencies that are already working with you.

Imagine this. You are standing in a room and you are kind of dirty. What we are doing is pointing you in the direction of the shower that's already operating. And once you're standing in the shower, you are reading a little manual on how to get clean, even though you're being cleaned. Now what this might show you is what it means to be clean and gaze upon yourself cleanly for the first time with an awareness of your clean self, but we are not the water that is running over you. We are an aspect of it, but the water is on all over the place.

When you understand that individual transformation is inexorably linked to mass transformation, you will begin to understand the significance of real change. When one person awakens to her Christed Self, she sets in motion a domino effect of resonance. One person says, "It is possible for me to lift my frequency and to exist at this level," and the person next to her goes, "Oh, really? I'm now starting to vibrate, too. I wonder why?" Now this is done without words. This is done in recognition of the frequency. If you have one high frequency and you place it next to one that is lower, the lower frequency then sees that it can go higher and attempts to resonate with the higher, and that is what is actually happening here. We're resonating at a high frequency. We're bringing this frequency to you and saying, "Yes, you can have it. It's here if you want it. Come on board, the view is much nicer from up here," so then you climb aboard through these exercises.

Now the vibration next to you is still vibrating at that frequency without the vocabulary or the focus or the exercises. But right now you have them. So when we speak of co-resonance and the individual change impacting the global change, it is really as follows: One person wakes up, the next person wakes up, they wake up ten, and a thousand, and on and on and on.

Now this is not done through religion. We want to be extremely clear about this. This is not religion. This is consciousness. Religion has been created as a manifesto individually for different groups to make changes in consciousness. Ultimately, the focus of all religions in truth, and the true religions, the religions that benefit spirit, are to bring up the frequency of those who engage in it. But the level of distortion that religion has received through acclimation to agendas, to politics and the use of fear to control those who would benefit from a shift in consciousness has gotten to the point where we must make this distinction. This is not about religion.

The world does not change because of a doctrine. A doctrine is a set of rules, if you think about it, and this is not a set of rules, it is a set of instructions that will align your frequency to the Christ vibration. The Christ vibration does not belong to Christians. Period. Do you understand this? The Christ vibration does not belong to one little group of people who believe the same thing. It is a frequency of consciousness that was manifested in form by Jesus and by others in different names over this time of history, over the last thousands of years. That is the truth.

Now when one group of people claims to have any answer that precludes other people from knowing something, you better watch out. If this book were to tell you that if you don't read this book, something dreary would happen to you, you'd better get another book very, very quickly, because that would be terrible instruction. And if any man tells you that the way to salvation, for lack of a better word, is their way and their way alone, run in the other direction today. And we say this with great seriousness. Run in the other direction today. Because that man is actually invested in control. There is no "my way or the highway" in consciousness.

The high road is a wide road and anybody is welcome to their consciousness at this frequency. It does not preclude them from having religion. Religion can be wonderful and on a personal level often is. The personal level that God exists in man is remarkable and truthful, and religion can give you the opening to an understanding of this, and then the individual experience is wonderfully transformed. So we are not knocking religion as a pathway, only the way religion can be and has been distorted over the millennium. Period.

So now, once you understand that your individual consciousness is being transformed through these energies that are acclimating the planet right now, and once you understand that this makes for change on individual consciousness and group experience, you can begin to understand a little more about what is transpiring on a global level. All of the groups are fighting who believe in separation. And this is, in some ways, the big hurrah for separation—just as you know when you have a pimple or a blemish or a boil, it will rise to the surface and break through the skin as it exits the body. And if you think of the body right now as the global matrix, these things are releasing in pockets of behavior and in crises and in planetary problems. And that is part of this shift. The old behavior has to leave. The sense of separation between men cannot be other than the separation between man and God.

The extent that man believes himself to be separate from his fellow man is the extent to which man believes he is separate from God. And even if he says, "I am doing this in the name of God," as he fights his brother, he is in illusion. And he is in deep illusion because he is empowering separateness.

So your duty as Christed Beings coming into consciousness is to change that in your own world. Once you do that, and once you change the belief that you are separate from your fellow man in your own world, you can begin to do it on a mass level on consciousness. This is a duty. This is a real duty.

Now a duty and a rule are two different things. We are simply telling you this. If you want to become Christed in your consciousness, you cannot include a belief in separation between men as part of that construct. It doesn't exist there. It's really like saying, "I am going to the Planet Mogo where there is no gravity," and you cannot expect gravity to exist there.

On the level of Christ consciousness, all men are one. All men are in beauty and perfection, and in different stages of realizing this. That does not mean that people don't act like jerks. They do. People are operating from all kinds of programming. Some of this is cultural, some of this is personal, some of this is nuts. People are doing all kinds of things. But that does not keep them out of this consciousness in your perception.

IF YOU SEE SOMEONE WHO IS ACTING POORLY AND YOU witness them in their Christ consciousness, you see them in their perfection, you are serving them at a very high level and giving them permission to transform. At the same time you don't have to support their behavior, which may be awful. No one is talking about a level of passivity that means people can walk all over you or do anything stupid.

We need you to understand this. When you say, "Turn the other cheek," you are not speaking about a physical response as much as you are speaking about a change in consciousness where what is slapped has no real meaning because the cheek does not burn on a level of consciousness. We will explain.

If you have an issue with your brother, and you are angry at your brother, and you send anger his way, that brother can turn the other cheek by rising in consciousness to a place where they cannot be struck by the energy that you are sending to them. It's really that simple. If you are vibrating at a higher frequency, you do not get zapped by the lower because, in fact, you have risen above it.

Paul is thinking, "Oh, is that the metaphor when people say to one another, 'Rise above it, you're better than that'?" Well, it's not that you're better than that, but you can "rise above it" quite literally, and when you do that in consciousness your experience changes, and the one who would smack you is just misguided. That doesn't mean you put up with it. But it does mean that you don't have to be in reaction and smack him back. Do you understand?

Now when we speak of truth, we speak of things that are

inexorable, things that do not change. And some things that do not change are facts like, "Energy does not leave, it only transforms," and when you change your energy, you are recreated. When you understand that on a level of consciousness all matter is frequency and this frequency manifests in different ways, you have an understanding of the process of creation, and you can create anything through your consciousness. This is actually a truth. Nothing can be created on this plane without a conscious intention to bring it forth. Anything that you see before you was actually created in consciousness. It was not an accident. It was created in consciousness. That is a truth.

Now another truth would be that you do not exist in a body only. And you have to get this for real before you go any farther. The misidentification with physical reality causes great fear, because everybody's frightened of losing what they have, and this includes the physical form that they live in. "What happens when my eyes go? What happens if I die? What happens if my feet don't work to take me where I need to go?" All fear-based thinking.

Once you understand that your physical body will not be here one day in its present form but you will exist in another form again and again and again, you have a much easier time being here because you don't have to hold on so tight. This is not your last meal. You don't have to stuff yourself and grab from your neighbor and feast until you're sick because there's nothing else coming. You have thousands of years and more and more and more of existence before you. And it will take different forms. And your consciousness, as you know it, will still be there in different ways, experiencing itself differently and learning. This is all about learning. So if you understand that you have a brunch waiting for you in the next lifetime, you don't have to pick at your neighbor's food and be frightened. Do you understand this? So you are eternal. You might as well get with the picture that's true. The picture is present, you are eternal with it, enough said.

Now the fear of death has a lot to it that we need to discuss with you as we approach the changes that you are undergoing. There are different kinds of death, and death, finally, is equated with transformation, a transitioning from one form into the next, because nothing truly dies. It is only transformed.

But there is a death of the ego self that we are going to address now because you might as well be prepared for what is to come. Now this is not a hard death, this is nothing terrible, nor is it even really a trial. It's simply a matter of outgrowing a personality self that has believed it would be in control for the rest of your existence. It's that simple.

Paul is seeing an image of a team leader in a summer camp who thought she would always get to be the team leader. And in fact, all the campers are growing up, and she can't lead them anymore because they've become smarter than she is.

So of course, she's going to panic. And she's going to try to control and get the campers to do what she wants on her last hurrah before she realizes that she doesn't have to do this, and that she can be higher in consciousness too, once she is absorbed by herself. And herself, on a true level, are the campers which she wishes to direct.

So we'll give you this example by saying, when the personality self realizes that she's out of ammunition and cannot run the show effectively anymore, she doesn't just walk away, she fights. And the ego that you have may put up a fight on its way out of its prominent role. You actually are not going to be walking around without a personality or without an ego. That would be impossible. But what you will be doing is operating from a dimensional level of Christ consciousness. And on that level, what is not truthful needs to fall away to let the light shine through you, and you become a vessel for spirit.

You are a vessel for spirit. You are precluded from that experience by the personality ego self, who decides what you should be for you. So that is the death, or the transition, that you are going to undertake. It's going to be about the release of the false self to allow your own light as the Christ consciousness to manifest through you fully. This is joyful. This is a course of wonder for all of you. And it is a process of acclimation and decision, as we have thus far described to you. But death of the personality self at the level that we are discussing must be understood simply as a transitioning and a re-appropriation of who you think you are.

If you have always thought that you were Fred and suddenly realize that you were adopted and your given name was Saul, suddenly you become Fred who was truly Saul. And in this case, you are really all the Christ consciousness. So it's really not that you haven't been Fred. That's a perfectly good name, but you're understanding who you really are in your heritage, in your truth, in your remarkable being. You are truly finding out that you are the Christ Self and you have believed yourself to be something minimal, something smaller or something that was ruled by an ego who thought she was the Big Kahuna, as it were. Now you can't be the Big Kahuna when you are the Christ because you become part of something much greater, and to the extent that you elevate yourself as "better than," you actually step outside of the Christ light and back into a fraudulent experience of religion. Do you understand this?

If you say you are something that you are not, you are lying. Now you may be misinformed, but to the extent that I say, "I am in the Christ," I am only speaking truthfully on the knowing level that I am this thing. I can say, "I am a man in a male body," and be speaking that truth, but I cannot say, "I am a fish," because I do not believe it. When you are in the Christ frequency, you need to be responding as such. So you cannot say, "I am better than Joe," "I am smarter than Frank," and "I am more wise than Peter." Because to an extent, when you are saying those things, you are putting yourself outside the relationship with these people that you would sort through in their Christ Selves. And that means this: Peter is as wise, Frank is as smart, etc. etc.

Everybody is the Christ manifesting in different ways. You do not expect Jimmy, who is three hundred pounds and beautiful, to be doing the high dive with the same grace as Genevieve, who has been swimming for years. But guess what? Everybody is capable of this movement. They are just at different stages of progression into their understanding of their Christed Selves.

So when you say, "I am better," meaning, "I am highly evolved," or "I am the Christ," and this is proclaimed with grandiosity, you are lying. You are not highly evolved. And in that moment, although your truth at a core level is your Christ, is yourself as Christ, your personality self has returned to dictate and is now misappropriating our teaching in the ways that religion has done to detriment for a long time.

When somebody says, "I have to go to the priest to be forgiven," they are endowing that priest with a power that is actually appropriated by that priest. And that priest, in fact, may be a wonderful priest and may actually be in consort and in alignment with the higher frequencies, but the moment the priest is judging, he is out of alignment. And really, you would have been much better going to the Source yourself anyway.

Any man, any woman is merely a conduit towards the divine. They can be a realized aspect of the divine in action, and we hope and pray that you become this through your experience of these energies, but there is a great difference between being a conduit and being the thing itself. And when people get confused and wind up in hospitals, it's because they think they are the king and not the servant of the king, as it were. Now we will explain what we mean.

To be the Christ means to be in the frequency of the Christ consciousness and to manifest the Self at that level. That is very, very different than deciding that you are the one doing this and that you can lay claim to that as a title at the exclusion of anybody else. When you do that, you are making yourself special and you are in your ego.

This is an admonition. Because your experiences are about to begin to transform through the work that you are undertaking, and while you will feel blessed and remarkable anyway through this achievement of consciousness and the gifts that make themselves available to you at this level, it actually is very different than saying, I am the gift, I am the gift, I am the blessing: "I am a conduit for this information. I am a piece of the Creator in action." Period.

Now we will go forward. We want to discuss a belief that Paul has been wondering about. And that is a belief in damnation. And that is a belief that you can be outside of God. Guess what, everybody? Nobody is damned. You are damned by yourselves through your own actions and the karma that you incur by them. But damnation is the wrong word for that. The true word, frankly, is learning. You are learning from your mistakes and your past actions and the karma that you incur through them. But nobody can be damned because God is with everybody.

Now Paul knows very well what it feels like to be on the outside. He had an experience when he was in his twenties of Christ consciousness that left him baffled and stunned for days. It was remarkable for him, and the sadness that overcame him that lasted for two years when that experience was ended was profound, because he believed himself, suddenly, to be outside a light that he had shown himself in spirit. He was shown his own self as the Christed energy for a brief time. Which means he felt a union. He felt the presence of the Christ, he felt at one, and then it was gone. So he mistakenly believed that he must have done something wrong, and that was not true. He simply had to transition to the next levels of consciousness in order to develop himself and that required work.

It's not a lot different than having a weekend in the sun and then going back to work in the office for a while until you have your next vacation, which is a new experience of the self in the higher frequencies. Each time you progress in the higher frequency, you retain the information and the consciousness that you have come to. Everybody, this is true. You don't lose your learning, it stays with you, and your abilities will be transformed by that understanding.

Now we want to get back to the idea that somebody can be without God. If you have the belief system that there is no God, that is your experience. If you want to believe that anything is your God, the power that you give that thing will create for you an experience of God. That is choice, that is why there can be many names and many kinds of God, but at the same time there really is one energy in total that is being addressed by you in prayer, in frequency.

You are one with the power and the frequency and the energy that created you, whether or not you believe it. So really, frankly, you cannot be outside of God. However, you can hold your consciousness at a low frequency through wrong thinking, through wrong belief systems, or through a belief in damnation that will keep you out of the light. You cannot believe that you have been damned and not act as if it's true. Guess what, everybody? It is not true. Nobody is outside of the light. They only believe they are. And that is great tragedy.

Paul, for a little while, has been seeing a figure that seems dark standing to the side. He is seeing this in his mind's eye and the figure looks sad and cloaked. And this is the self, the aspect of the self that believes, on some sad level, that he is damned or is not allowed entry into the light.

We all have aspects of the self that we believe are dirty or wrong or shameful, or we all have things that we have done that we believe would create unforgiveness of us if it were truly known. And that is the image that Paul is seeing: that aspect of a self that believes himself to be outside of the light. So we wish to do an exercise with you now.

We want you to sit and we want you to think of a time when you felt that you were outside of God or the light or you felt, quite simply, that you could not be forgiven for something that you have done. Now we don't want you to sit in this energy long, we simply want you to remember it.

And now we want to bring in a light. And this is the Christ light. And we want to bring this through you and around you, above you and below you. And we want to enfold you in the Divine Light of the Christ frequency.

"I am Word through my belief that I may now be forgiven for anything real and imagined. And I now allow that aspect of myself that believes that he is outside of the light to be embraced by the light and transformed in the light of the Creator. I am Word through this intention. Word I am Word."

Now to do this daily with yourself will actually bring you into alignment on a higher frequency, but it's not required. We simply want to show you that those aspects of the self that you believe to be outside of God's love can be brought into it through your intention and through the action of the Word.

The extent that you do not forgive your brothers is usually a strong indication of the lack of self-forgiveness that you hold. And we can tell you this. You might as well start forgiving yourself now for anything you believe you have done. We have examined this already in an earlier chapter, but we know that for you it is a process. Yet still we say, you might as well start forgiving yourself now, because the freedom that you will experience will be wonderful, and it is your birthright to understand yourself as in God's love.

So back to damnation. It's a false belief. Period. Man cannot be put outside of God because God is everything. God is the frequency of every cell in your being. You are vibration. You are an aspect of the Creator, nothing else. Period. Word I am Word.

Now we want to tell you something. What we want to tell you is your choice to believe that you are working on this project of yourself coming into alignment with the Christ truth is significant, not only for you in this time, but significant for everybody else in frequency.

We have discussed earlier the concept of co-resonance, and now we want to take it even a step further: that the matrix of this planet that has been held in fear, that is now shifting is also impacted by the grid of light that is being developed by those of you who are elevating in consciousness. And the higher this grid is aligned to, and the more people that are waking up to their own divinity and to their own aspect of the Christ Self in manifestation, the more light there is available on this planet for the dimensional shifts that occur.

So in some way you become beacons of light that guide the energies to you that can bring forth the changes that are required on this plane. You are each doing this work if you wish, and it is big work. Now when we say "beacon," we mean a beam of light that attracts to it that which it needs and guides others through its focus.

The more focused you are in your intention right now to become into alignment with your Christ Self, the more focus you have as a frequency and the higher you rise. Paul is wondering if there is energy work to be done to help you sort out what you are really doing in this process. And we say, "Yes, there is," and we will commence with it now.

You are a beam of light, sitting under a tree. Think of this, please. You are contemplating yourself as a beam of light and this light is extending around you and higher and higher and higher. And as you sit under this tree in contemplation, the wisdom of your true identity as a Christed Being is manifested in you. And the light that you are rises and grows to meet with all the other lights that are blossoming and beaming and growing on this plane of existence. And as you greet the other lights, you shift in your consciousness to an awareness of your duty as a Christed soul and a beacon of light who will herald the dawn of this new frequency on this plane. Period.

Paul is saying, "What about a new frequency? This isn't a new frequency, is it?" No, it is not a new frequency, but it is newly being brought forth at this time to acclimate to you, to those around you, and to the planetary grid that is currently in transformation. The Christ frequency and the Christ consciousness is eternal, but we are activating you anew and that is what we mean. We will explain anything you wish. When you have questions, you must learn to ask.

Now we want to take a break for a moment and discuss something very different. We want to discuss attitude. And attitude is a personality construct but is also a vehicle of your expression, and when you express yourself, you are expressing your frequency. When you express negativity, you are expressing a negative frequency. When you discuss your brother in a lower way, you are abiding in that frequency and you are attempting to bring that frequency to your fellow in a way that is not constructive. If you decide about somebody, and that somebody is a certain way and cannot be changed, you are actually in heresy. And we mean it this way: "That guy's a jerk. He will never change," decides, in that moment, that you are the Creator and you know what is going to happen to him.

How can you know that? When you go back to the Bible, there was an awakening on the road to Damascus where one soul was transformed into an awakening. Anything can happen to anybody. So the moment you decide that someone is resolved, cannot be changed, will not change, you decide in a moment that you are God and you are judging your brother. And in that moment you step outside of the Christ frequency, you lower your own frequency and to a certain extent you stop being a conduit, because the Christ frequency cannot flow through you when you are in judgment of your fellow man. Period.

So we decide today that we are only going to hold those attitudes which are productive to the alignment to the new frequency that is available to you. If you wish to decide now that you will not speak ill of your brother, you will have an interesting day, because you are going to catch yourself many, many times attempting to do just that. "Old habits die hard" is truthful. However, if you intend at this time to preclude negativity as an aspect of your personality, we will support you in this.

Paul is acting surprised. "Does this mean I can say, 'Word I am Word' through my personality self and move forward with a better personality?" *Better* is not the right word. A frequency expressed through the personality is always a frequency expressed through the personality. However, when you are aligning to the higher frequencies, it's a little productive and more than a little beneficial to state this intention:

"I am Word through my intention to hold my brothers in high regard. I am Word through my intention to realize the perfection that is created in all men. I am Word through the attitudes and personality traits I have developed in such a way that they will reflect my new awareness of my brother's divinity and the divinity that is inherent in all things. Word I am Word through this intention. Word I am Word."

We are wondering now if you wish to do something a little bit different. We are wondering if you are willing to take an exercise to your fellows in a practical way. We are going to ask you this: What would it be like to sit opposite someone and claim to them in your consciousness, "I am Word through this one before me"? See what you do when you do this exercise with a fellow. Sit opposite him and state this intention:

"I am Word through my fellow. I am Word through the one before me. I am Word through Joe or Jane or Bill [or whatever name the name is of the partner you choose]. I am Word through the one before me."

We wish you to do this and to begin to understand that when you are working in frequency, you are working actively. Everything that we are teaching you in this book is energy activation or is used to lift your consciousness so that you may have access to your own frequency at the higher dimension available to you now. We want you to understand that this is not just about talk and language. This is about frequency that can be felt and experienced in a practical way. So saying, "I am Word through the one before me," will give you the first inclination of what you can do.

When you state this for your friend, you do this with the intention to allow the Word to work through them. And as you do this, you need to feel what you feel in your own body, in your own energy frequency. And your friend needs to also feel what happens in her body and her frequency, and then you may discuss this.

What most of you will experience is a heightening and a lifting in the frequency that you are in and your friend will experience something similar. We will talk to you more about what this means in further chapters.

We want to leave you today with a vision. And this is the vision: We want you to see yourself standing on a ship. And this ship is crossing the sea. And as you are on this ship, the waves are rising and falling. But you are always supported in the vessel that you are traveling in. And as the ship nears its shore, you understand that you are moving towards a new vision of yourself and a full experience of yourself as the Christed being that you are in truth. You stand on this shore, a new man, a new being, a new self in an understanding of "I am Word."

"Word I am Word through this intention to realize myself as Word. Word I am Word."

Thank you and goodbye.

March 10, 2009

We're ready for this. We've been waiting for a day to resume the last lecture, and this is going to be the end of the last lecture in some ways, and we will start the next chapter when we are ready to.

Decision making is coming for you all, decisions about what you want for yourself and how you will get what you want. This is going to be happening on a cultural level, a countrywide level, and a planetary level. Everybody is making decisions about what they want as they adjust to the higher frequencies that are permeating the energy field of this planet. And that involves restructuring the grid of your reality.

When you make a choice that is based in the reality that you have known in the past, you are recreating a pattern based on your understanding from the past. However, you cannot do that when you enter the new realm of energy that is present for you now. It doesn't work. You cannot wear the same clothing in the Arctic that you can on the beach because the climate has changed and the frequency is changed and, consequently, to put on the old clothes by way of decisions would not work well any more than putting on a hat when you mean to take one off. You are all in a change pattern right now and you are going to understand this more as the months and years progress. But the gift of this time is about relinquishing the past.

Relinquishing the past involves many, many things, including a lack of response to those things that you believed that you would never have to let go of. If you're always frightened of losing something, you can guarantee you are going to lose it. Understand, though, that the requirements of change don't necessarily mean that you have to divest yourself of anything that you have created that is to your benefit unless it is time for it to leave because it no longer resonates with who you are becoming. Do you understand this? To imagine the self in a static frequency for an eternity is mind boggling. As your frequency changes, you must express it. And as you express it, you are required to make choices. As you make these choices, your environment and your landscape has to be acclimated to the frequency that you are in now, because this is the place where these choices are being made. As they are made, you change everything. Period.

Changing everything. What does that feel like to you when you say it? "I am changing everything." Some of you may feel free. Others of you will panic. And we want to again tell you that when we say changing everything you must not think in practical ways as much as you must understand that it is your consciousness that is transformed, and your consciousness is what is rendered through this work to out-picture itself in form, in physical manifestation. So nothing is bad. You don't create negativity or lack or fear when you move into the higher realms. Why would that even be possible? Why would you undertake this work only to find yourself sitting on a street corner begging for food? That makes no sense at all.

So please understand when you teach this frequency through your life and through your actions, you are speaking only of powerful manifestation of the Christ frequency and that brings good. That brings good. That brings good.

Now don't fear yourselves as you undergo these changes. That's the big problem here, really. You're frightened of yourselves, and you're frightened that you can't do what you need to do in order to empower yourself to make things better when they don't seem to be connecting. When things don't seem right. When things aren't happening the way you thought that they should. And then you disempower yourself in your fear or, worse still, you begin to take actions based on that fear and when you do that, you create things in fear. When you create something in fear, you'll have something that you're going to then need to release.

You have heard the stories about the little boy who tells the lie and the lie grows and grows and grows and grows. And to a certain extent, the boy who cried wolf created a terror that was worse than the real thing, because he created a fabrication and it made itself real. Do you understand this?

So when you create something in fear, you create something that you will then need to dismantle in consciousness because ultimately you can't live with it. It can't last anymore. It is navigating itself away from you. And "Navigation" is going to be the title of this chapter. Navigation. We are going to say navigation, now, because it's about steering a boat, and we left you on a boat, quite happily, yesterday, pulling up to a new shore. And that was a principle we were giving you. That you ride a choppy sea in a vessel that stays calm, and then you embark on the next leg of your voyage.

Your voyage is present now. You are already standing on the dock having made the decision to take this journey. And you are traveling. And you are traveling and you are resolved to get to the other shore. Now we're not going to give you a directive on navigating a boat any more than we are navigating your self through your taxes, or your marriage, or your thoughts about anything right now. We are going to simply tell you that when you are in navigation in the higher realms, you are being directed in your consciousness by your higher knowing.

So today we want to talk about higher knowing and what this really means. We are going to decide now that the next chapter begins at this point.

EIGHT

I AM IN MY KNOWING

March 10, 2009

"I Am in My Knowing" is my name as a chapter. "I Am in My Knowing." And we want you to repeat this as often as you can. Once you are in your knowing, you begin to accomplish things that you could not have otherwise, because understand that the level of fear that precludes you from your knowing takes up most of your energy. Now you all understand what it means to feel yourself as being in your knowing. To be in your knowing means that you resonate truthfully and you don't question what you feel. It is the truth and it is unshakable in your system because you understand that.

Now to operate from your knowing is very different than walking down a block knowing that the post office box where you drop your bills is waiting for you. That's just clear direction. But for all you know, really, while you were sleeping somebody moved the darned box. So that's not a really good example of knowing. A real example of knowing is to be able to say to yourself, "I am in my self. I am in my knowing as my self," because your self is the one thing that will not transform on a true level. And we speak of your self as your essence, as your Christed Self. You are eternally you at this level.

"I know that spring comes" is not a real belief system to claim, because for all you know something may happen and spring may not arrive as planned. You may be vacationing someplace where it is a blizzard outside. Guess what? You would have been wrong in your knowing. So we want to get past the little things that you believe you know to get to the big stuff that we can then anchor in for you in terms of your ability to know yourself at this level of consciousness.

Now when you ask yourself, "What am I?" your first inclination is to say, "I am Paul, I am Victoria, I am Mark, I am John, I am Bill," whatever you want to say. You have named yourself, and you carry that name through this lifetime unless you decide to change it to something else. You don't appliqué a new name on your jacket unless you want to be identified as Natasha when your real name is Kim. You just don't do it. So you accept that you are Kim, and whatever your name is, that is the first level of self-identification you work with. But your name, frankly, although it carries with it an energy and a resonance, is not your true self. It's the tag that you use to navigate yourself through this lifetime. You will take it off at the end of this lifetime like a bracelet and you will assume a new one when you come back. But on a higher level you do have a name encoded in you, which is the cellular identification of yourself as a soul, a Christed soul on its way back to the Creator.

So when we say to you, "I am Word," we are actually telling you that that is your name. That is your name. That is your name. You can call it Yahweh, you can call it by any golden name you wish to, but in essence we are all saying, "I am one with my Creator and I am journeying to my place of unification with that consciousness. As I identify with that aspect of the self that is the Creator, I rise in frequency and the journey commences quickly." Period.

So we are telling you now that your identity is not something that you know on this level until you claim it. When you claim it, you begin to integrate it. No mumbo jumbo here. When you claim you are the Word, you identify with the aspect of the self that you truly are eternally. And this you can know.

When you operate from this knowing, you begin to achieve something that we are working with you each, and that is a claim to your persona as a vested being in the light. When we say this, we actually mean that your identification beyond personality comes to the forefront so that you can serve as you would, a teacher, or a light, and you can act in response to this energy as a willing emissary. This means, finally, that you cannot be passive once you are in this frequency. It's not about sitting in your apartment identifying as the light. That's rather comfortable, don't you think? But ultimately the light does what it needs to do to serve the source of the Great Light.

Now we want to be very clear with you. This does not mean that you attach the idea of service in ways that are culturally appropriate to you. Sometimes people believe that if they are in service to the Christ or in the light and in service to the action of the light, they have to hang a shingle outside their door, or they have to serve food, or they have to become missionaries. And these are all wonderful, wonderful callings. However, the uniqueness that is you, that creates itself through you in the Christ, wants to be magnified through the gifts that you have inherited or you have come to or you have gained through your practice of existing in human consciousness. So if you are a painter, paint away, enjoy yourself, but you will be doing this as this energy. And if you are a singer, you will sing and if you are taking out the garbage for a living, that will be your joy if that gives you the sense of truth that your work is right for who and what you are.

You have the choice here. Now God does not decide one day that Frank is going to be a missionary any more than he decides that Sheila is going to be a temporary worker in an office. That's not something that is decided on a higher level. However, you each have journeys and you are part of the navigation of them from birth because you are always creating. So the reason that you took the job in the temporary agency that placed you in the office may be to teach you a skill that you will use years later when you are doing something quite different. You have no idea how these things unfold until you realize how wonderfully informed you have been by your past experiences. You can be a garbage man of great dignity and actually have a life of the mind that has nothing to do with trash cans. But that is a wonderful way to work out the anger at the end of the day by throwing the bags into the back of the truck. And you are helping people.

Now of course we sound somewhat simplistic in our examples, but we are only trying to tell you that when you navigate your life, much of what you create is for reasons you don't understand at the time, but you may understand it very much later when it comes into operation in a way of service. So we say you're all going into service of some kind as you work with this frequency.

There is a dilemma for some of you that means, "If I do this, that means I have to relinquish the ideals or the goals or the beliefs I have about who I am supposed to be." Yes, that's true, you will release these beliefs. But the goals may be valid and they may be wonderful and why would service preclude you from realizing your goals in achievement? Nobody takes anything away from you.

So we want to talk now about truth in your knowing and

what this really means. When you are in your truth, you are knowing. You do not know when you are not in your truth. If you can understand as much as anything that it is raining outside and you are wet, you know you are in your truth. There is no conjecture, you are all wet. If you are crying and there are tears running down your face, you can say, "I am in my tears, I am crying." That is a truth. Or standing on the grass. Or kissing a friend. Or holding a child. These are the truths because they are what you are engaged with fully in the moment they are being experienced. That is what you know. And your knowing must be anchored into present time for it to be valid.

We gave you an example a few days ago about people believing that the world was flat. And they knew the world was flat because that's what they believed. Now that has been dismantled as a belief system. But in your case you believe what you don't know to be true still because you accept it. So we are telling you right now, knowing happens in the present moment. You can't know something yesterday and tomorrow. You know it in the present moment.

Now we want to do an exercise with you that will anchor your knowing into you in a way that becomes truthful, which means you will feel it, you will claim it, and you will know it. And we ask you now to align to the vibration of the Word by saying:

"I am Word through my body. Word I am Word. I am Word through my vibration. Word I am Word. I am Word through my knowing of myself as Word."

Now we tell you this. In your mind, we want you to go back to a time when you knew something as a truth. "I know I am a writer." "I know I love my husband." "I know my child is sick with the flu." "I know that the world is a safe place." "I know that I am loved." You can choose your knowing. But go into that place of knowing and feel that knowing in your heart or in your energy system. It does not really matter what you choose to know. We only want you to feel it. To feel what it means to be in the vibration and experience of your knowing. So, yes, this is what you do now: "I am in my knowing. Word I am Word."

Once this is expressed, you are actually bringing energy to support this fact. And when you do this, you can begin to realize what you know. So once you have anchored in the memory of your knowing, we want you now to decide something that you need to know. "I need to know if I am on the right path in my life." "I need to know if the job I am in is secure." "I need to know if I love the man I say I love." Ask the question now. "I am Word through my knowing. Word I am Word," and begin to resonate as you did the first time with the response that you receive. Feel what you feel. Let your heart teach you. Let your knowing be present. We are taking you out of our head and into your frequency and out of the brain and into the heart center. "I am in my knowing. Word I am Word."

Once you can begin to anchor in the experience of knowing, you can begin to work with it consciously, and once you know once, you know, period. It's like anything else. When those of you who have had an experience of the Creator relive that experience, there is only a shadow left. There is a memory of the glory that you experienced when you felt yourself at one with the Christ or with the Universe. There is a wonderful memory, but it is a shadow, however you knew when it was happening how powerful it was.

If you remember the first time you met your love and you knew this was your love, you can resonate with that. The love may have passed or have been changed, but you know what it means to know. Now once you know, you can begin to act from your action in the knowing that you have. Once you do this once, you can do it again and again and again. And what we mean by this is, "I can be in my knowing and act on that knowing with purpose and understanding that I am safe."

We will tell you this. When you are in your knowing, you are not afraid. You know it. You know the truth and there is no fear in that kind of truth. You will feel this in your heart. When you are in your knowing, you understand that you are safe and the actions that you take from this place of knowing will bring you benefit. When you are acting from your fear, you create more fear and you entangle yourself in distrust and other problems that will manifest from that creation, but when you are in your knowing, you are safe.

So right now we would like you to decide that your knowing is accessible to you on a deeper level. You will decide this. You will change a pattern that you have lived with your entire life with this action, because up until now you did not know you could know.

"I am knowing myself as a piece of the Creator. I am Word through this knowing. Word I am Word. I am knowing myself as a Divine Being. Word I am Word through this intention. Word I am Word. I am knowing my actions. I am knowing my needs. I am knowing the requirements for my growth. I am knowing what is needed to bring me to this next level of frequency and I am honoring my knowing every moment of every day. I am Word through this intention. Word I am Word."

What we have done right now is to magnify something that was present. And you understand that to magnify means to make bigger. Your knowing was always present, but if you can imagine a great big magnifying glass above it helping it to grow into form, that is essentially what is happening in your energy field through these intentions that you just set.

Once again we tell you this is not abracadabra. This is an intention that is set in consciousness and activated through the Christ frequency that you have become aligned to through the reading and actions, information available to you through this text as well as the planetary frequency that is embarking on this great change.

Everyone is changing. And we will remind you again that you are part of this, but the only difference right now is you are being given a vocabulary and a manual of how to understand the changes that you may be experiencing and how to work with the frequencies on a much more direct level than you would have otherwise. The text is a manifestation of this energy, and frankly you could actually "feel" the book as much as read it and acquire benefits from the information on that level. We are not talking magic, we are talking frequency. Everything has a frequency. Everything vibrates at a different level, and the text that you are working now with has its own frequency. Period.

Now we will tell you this. Encoded in your being are the instructions for your own transformation. This is in the DNA of every man and woman. This is an aspect of who you are. And Paul is saying, "Physical DNA, or are you talking metaphorically?" We will say yes, metaphorically and physically. Because the body has to realign to the higher energies as it moves forward in its evolution, and in this stage of the game mankind is unraveling some dense energies that have precluded the awareness of his abilities as a frequency being. And we've started to tell you about this already.

To serve as a vehicle for this frequency will then begin to teach you what the frequency needs to be in service. So we gave you examples of sponsors, energies that work with you to align you and teach you what you need. And we spoke to Paul about manifestation of the abilities of consciousness, which we will again say are clairaudience, clairvoyance, clairsentience. These are ways people can begin to experience energies at a higher frequency.

We want to say something to you now that's quite important. Psych-ism is ability as much as anything else. And we are not talking about seeing ghosts or reading tarot cards. Those are things people do, but that is not part of this teaching. What is part of this teaching is an expansion of your awareness in consciousness to enable you to work with the abilities we have described in ways that are practical and will be of service to your own growing awareness and to those you would work with.

We want to go farther with this right now. We want to tell you that the experience of feeling frequency enables you to anchor in the frequency only because you have had a practical experience of the other realms. We will give you an example. If you don't believe in something, telling you something is true may make a dent in your consciousness but not nearly as much as having your own experience of it. The work we've done with Paul has been very physical. He didn't believe in much, so one day he asked to believe, and he got to see frequency enough to enable him to go on a journey to find out what the heck he was seeing. When you start seeing lights around people, you get worried and you want to have an answer.

Now your experiences, your own experiences of the dense vibrations, need to be transformed, but we don't want to teach you an exercise that's really about playing at an ability. We want you to have the ability in ownership and through your own experience. And the quickest way that we can do this is to support you in your owning that it is possible for you to develop your abilities in consciousness so that you can work with them directly in a way that will give you the clarification or the proof that you require of yourself as a frequency submitting itself as part of a Great Frequency in consciousness.

What you are saying is, "I am willing to know what I am made of. I am willing to have an experience of it that is tangible to me on a physical level or on a level that is appropriate to my learning." Many of you, if you felt energy for the first time in a very direct way, would become frightened. You would say, "Something's happening to me, and I don't trust it." And because of that, you will not have that level of experience, because it's not appropriate to you. Someone else may say, "I want it to come in a dream because I love my dreams and it's a place for me to learn," and guess what? That's where you're going to have your experience.

But we will tell you this. If you want the development of your skills, of your abilities in manifestation, you can ask for them now. And to the degree that you are willing to transform yourself to enable these gifts to come to the forefront, you will get them. We will say this to you now. If you chose this, you are going to have to unblock the mechanisms, the dense energies that have kept them in place, but that can be done quite simply now.

Paul is seeing a seal, the vision of a seal, imprinted over his forehead. And this is an image of a seal being broken over a chakra that has been held. The chakra, in this case, is the chakra of sight that will allow the clairvoyant sight to begin to be made manifest. So we ask you this. Would you now be willing to align to the possibility that the seal that is over your sixth chakra, anything that is obstructing you from owning your own abilities to see energy in the way that is appropriate to you, will now be cleared from you in safety and in peace? If you affirm this, you will set in motion the passage of energy release that is required to bring this into being:

> "I am Word through this intention to release the blocks that may be inhibiting my second sight. Word I am Word through this intention. Word I am Word."

We say "second sight" because it's not an inappropriate term. You see with your physical eyes and you see with your third eye as well. And you will manifest this transformation that you have decided on in ways that are appropriate to you.

Now we are not telling you that if you don a grass skirt, you become a hula dancer. This isn't saying that at all, nor does this mean that you are going on a big ghost hunt. What it means is you have set in motion a release of energy and belief systems that are attached to those energies that have precluded you from utilizing an ability that is present in all men. Period. If you want to go see auras, go see auras, but you are not going to see them until the third eye opens up and clears itself at the level that is required for your sight to begin to unfold. We have just supported you in this action, so trust it. Now we want to move on.

The ability to feel energy happens to you anyway and we've discussed this in a previous chapter. Yesterday we told you it would be a good idea to sit again with a colleague, with a fellow, and claim, "I am Word through my fellow. I am Word through this one before me." If you did this, you have had an experience twice now of opposite experience with someone in a vibration that we claim to be Word. The first time you did it, you did it with an intention to experience the energy. The second time you did it, it was actually informed by the teachings that followed, and we hope that you have had a slightly different experience of the energies of Word.

When you say, "I am Word," and you bring the energy through your fellow, you are actually activating them, and we have discussed this already. But we want you to understand that when you feel somebody else's energy, you will feel it in your own energy system.

Now this is a little bit different. If you feel John's arm with your hands, you reach across to John and you feel what it feels like. You express yourself through touch, and the arm is a physical thing. However, when you are feeling somebody in energy, you are feeling your arm as their arm, so frankly, it's a little confusing to the unanointed, and you wonder why you feel a backache when you sit next to your aunt Sarah and you're vibrating at a high frequency. More than likely, Aunt Sarah has a bad back and you are attuning to it. When you begin to vibrate as a healer, you vibrate at a higher frequency, and the healing frequencies go to work. So your aunt Sarah may be benefiting enormously by sitting beside you, because she may be getting the energy she requires on a causal level to support her in transforming the pattern that created the backache. But we said when you are sitting opposite your fellow, what you might feel will be in your own system, so you have to understand that your own system is something that you need to begin to monitor. You need to begin to monitor how you feel in your physical being and what radiates around you.

So for a moment now, sit quietly and we will tell you what

we would like you to do. And then you will put the book down and you will do it.

We want you to sit back with your eyes closed and feel yourself as energy. "What do I feel like now? What do I feel like? What is moving in me? What is moving around me?" And then we would like you to feel this energy extend around you, in your aura, so that you are actually feeling your energy frequency surrounding you, a large field of light. We want you to feel your aura. Feel what it extends to. How does it feel to inhabit yourself in your aura to this extent?

We would like you to do this every day. We would like you to acclimate to this, to understanding your own frequency. Now when you say, "I am Word through my frequency," or "I am Word through my energy field," you will begin to feel the difference because you will begin to feel the acclimation of your own frequency to the energy field around you. You are changing, and you will feel this through your own energies.

As you become aware of what your own frequency is, you become more comfortable experiencing the energies of others in direct ways. You also become more attuned to the information that their energy systems will be offering you. Some of this will be coming as a knowing and you will know things about people. Some of it will be coming as feeling and you will feel things for people, about people, what they are feeling emotionally or what is in their bodies. And some of it will come through what you see.

When you begin to see energy, the first thing you will think is that your eyes are playing tricks on you. And that is because you have been seeing energy your whole life and you've been feeling like your eyes were playing tricks on you. So we have to understand that once you understand that this is not anything other than a capability that you have not used and you have misunderstood, we can make progress in your own sight.

So we will tell you this: We invite you now to go out to someplace where there are people and there is quiet. And this can be a restaurant. It can be a twelve-step meeting. It can be a class. It can be an office. It does not really matter. But we want you to be in your frequency in an expanded state. Feeling your frequency around you. And we want you to see the ones before you.

You can choose one person if you wish. And you will see them. And you will invite yourself to begin to see them as frequency. You do not do this through effort, you do this through intention. When you do this, of course, your eyes will be relaxing and you will be allowing the energies to make themselves known to you psychically through the third eye that we have decided is now going to be unblocked. You may first see a small field of energy vibrating very quickly around a part of the body, and then another. But you may see a large expanse of energy. Distance is supportive of this when you are first beginning to see. And seeing from a distance will allow you to relax your eyes, to unfocus them, to begin to experience the energy field of your subject.

We would like you to do this once a day and see the differences as you begin to journey into this realm of understanding energy in a practical way. We are talking practically here. We want you to have an experience that you can lay claim to. Beyond deciding that the text is truthful, we have said to you again and again that this work must be experiential, so we want you to experience and that will align your knowing.

Now we want to tell you some things about your jurisdiction as a soul. You cannot control other people. It cannot happen. And to misuse energy through intention is a misalignment and a misappropriation of frequency. So we require you now to decide once and for all that you're not even going to attempt it.

We said earlier in the book that the vibration of the Word cannot be misused. But when you begin to access information on people's issues or energy fields, you become privy to information that your conscious mind would not ordinarily receive. And this is a responsibility. You do not want to run up to Cousin Sheila and say, "Your back is out." You don't want to do it. You want to say, "How's your back doing?" if that's the most that needs to be said. But for the most part, at this stage of the game, we are actually asking you only to become aware. We are not asking you to take action. This is not a book in psychic development. We simply speak of the abilities that make themselves known as you begin to transform your frequency.

We would like to take a few questions now on the material that we have given you to date and we invite Victoria to speak if there are things she would like further clarification on.

"I am Word through this intention, Word I am Word, to know what I need to know in order to bring my information to me in ways that are perfect for my unfoldment. Word I am Word."

So be it. Ask questions if you wish.

VN: Okay, here's a question to the guides. Were you once human?

No we were not. Some of us were in form, and personality was activated, but ultimately we are teachers and we are not coming from this plane of existence. We have manifested right now as frequency and consciousness and we do not exist in form. We existed in form in some ways, at different times, and we have inhabited form. But we are not dead people come back through a tape device speaking to Paul. Do you understand this?

VN: Yes.

Question?

VN: And I guess the question after that is, in what relation do you stand to God?

We are part of God. We are of the essence of God. As you get closer to the frequency of the Godhead you vibrate in accordance with God. So we know ourselves as light and consciousness and of God. But we will not tell you we are that, any more than we will tell you that you are that. We are both that. We are all that. But we are aspects of the Creator manifesting Himself as consciousness. Period.

VN: And the third and last question, then, is what is God?

God is the source. God is the great source. God is the frequency and the energy that joyfully permeates all matter. God is everything. God is everything. God is everything. And we say this with joy. Word I am Word. So be it. Word I am Word.

Thank you both and stop.

We have completed this chapter for today; we will give you titles for former chapters as we continue. We are grateful for your presence and for your industry and we ask only that you trust this exchange to the extent that you do to show up and be present and aligned. We will take care of the rest. You are in service and we are in service and this is an act of giving for all. We thank you both and we attend now to the light. Word I am Word. Goodbye now.

March 11, 2009

We're ready for the talking now. And we want to talk about where we were yesterday with the pronouncement, "I am in my knowing." And what "I am in my knowing" signifies is the responsibility for your own information. When you are in your own information, you are owning yourself as a conscious being who is directed by himself in alignment with his higher knowing. Now once you are in your higher knowing, you begin to respond to it a little bit differently than you would normally, and we will tell you simply that this has to do with actions that are motivated by truth. And actions that are motivated by truth in your knowing will bring you to a new place and also bring you forward to a different space of understanding.

When you take an action from your truth, you are always moving yourself forward. Now you can ask yourself, "Does that include the little things? When I know I'm hungry and I get dinner, is that bringing me forth into new truth?" No, not really. But when you know in your heart that you are ready for something new, you will call to you those experiences that will bring you to what you need to further your growth. When you act on that knowing and you move forward, you are aligning yourself once again to frequency at a higher level. This is the process of forward motion. So we want you to be responsive to what you know and how you know it and what it means to be in your knowing.

Yesterday we gave you an exercise that would amplify your knowing. We said to feel something that you knew, to feel it fully and then to amplify that knowing throughout your energy field so that you could resonate with the consciousness of knowing. Now already you question yourself: "Did I do it right? Did I operate from my knowing when I got the exercise? Was I supported in my understanding of this or did I just not get it at all?"

Now that's all okay. But we will tell you this. To bypass your own knowing is to continue to keep yourself without awareness of your power and ability. So we have to put you in your knowing regardless of how much doubt you bring to it. Once you know something, it is in resonance with you. The energies of doubt collude with fear to keep you disempowered from yourself in your mastery, and in your mastery means in your consciousness as a realized man, woman, being. Period.

When you are in your consciousness, in your knowing, what you are capable of is transforming to you and to your life and is of benefit to others. Period. When you know who you are at a deep level, you are in your integrity always. You are always operating from that place of consciousness that states its own awareness of its worth. "I am in my knowing" is only true to the extent that the depth of the knowing is incorporated of that aspect of the self that is truthfully conscious and aware of himself as a Christed Being.

Now you don't need to use that language per se to have this experience. You can be in a country where the belief systems are completely different, but the truth would be the same. That in your essence, your Christed Self is an aspect of the divine operating within you, and that that aspect of the self known to you as your truth and as your essence will always ground you in your honor and in your worth because it cannot do otherwise. When you understand that, you have a clear anchor to your response to any question about your worth that you could ever have.

Paul keeps seeing a well. He sees the image of a well, but he doesn't see what's at the base of it. We will explain the image he is seeing to him.

He is seeing a well because at the depth of his being is this well of consciousness, of a soul understanding of who he is, and what he is. Now we want to bring the water of the well up. Up, up, up, up, up to the surface so that he may wash himself in it. And this is an exercise we will do with you each:

Imagine that you see a well, a deep well, and the water is rich and it is light and it is wonderful and it glimmers at the base of the well. And as the well rises, you reach into it with both your hands and you bring the water to your face. You drink from this well and you anoint yourself with the deep waters that have come to meet you.

When you do this, you are simply claiming your own consciousness has risen to meet you in present time. It's a simple illustration of calling to you the information you need on a level of consciousness to require your response to this information. And that means you can drink from your own information, you can be anointed in your own light, you can call to you the water of Christ that you need. Period.

Now we will go back to your knowing and its establishment in your consciousness. Now we tell you this. When you are established in your consciousness, you regard yourself differently. There are certain things that you don't engage in. One of them is approval, and the requirements of approval that you may have foisted on yourself or been gifted with culturally, or by your fellows, or your family.

The need to be approved of actually vanishes when you are in your knowing at the frequency that we speak of. And the reason is very simple. There is nothing to be gained from it. You are not looking for affirmation for yourself from outside of you because it's not required. The well that is you is full. You do not need to have it from another source.

So we say to you this. Your desire to have approval from another party at this present time, although it can be helpful as a way of gauging your process, or gauging your relationship, or assuming your relationship through response, is not something that you will require when you move forward in consciousness. So we want you to do a little exercise with us now.

We want you to imagine that you stand in a room full of people. And you are regarding them as the ones who know. They know more than you do. They all know more. Perhaps they have achieved the things that you believed you were supposed to have achieved. Or perhaps they have information that you believe is what you need to move forward in your life. What does it feel like to be in relationship to them? What do you want from them? How do you feel about yourself? Do you stand alone? Do you run to them with questions? How do they regard you? To what extent do you feel disempowered by your own lack of knowing in the company of those who know?

Some of you may feel like an eager student. But the majority of you probably will just feel unapproved of, and less than, and like there must be some mistake that you can even be in their company because you are not approved of.

Now we want to reverse this little exercise. And we want you to stand in the same room and be the one who is in his knowing surrounded by people who don't know and require your approval. What does this feel like to be the one in power? To be the one in consciousness? Do you feel like a sage? Do you feel like a teacher? Or do you just feel like there's a lot of people around you who for some crazy reason think you know more than you do?

We are not talking about informational knowing now. We are talking about approval. An external realization and affirmation of the self as brought through your relationship with others. We want you to understand at this moment that eighty percent of what you are doing in your life has been motivated by a need for approval from someone else, or a cultural belief that what you need to do is a certain thing, or by a certain time. You have these beliefs and you operate with them as if they are truths.

How can you be in your own knowing when you are operating from truths that are misaligned to your requirements for growth? How can you be knowing what you need on a conscious level, a truly conscious level, when you think instead of know? And you think you are supposed to have a certain income, or a certain level of respect, or a certain kind of spouse, or a certain meditation practice, or a certain church, or a certain relationship with your sister, or your husband, or your own body.

You have all of these things that are inherited belief

systems and you do them for approval as much as anything else, because quite consciously you can't imagine yourself as operating outside of that field of information. You believe yourself to be part of community to the extent that you go where you're told to go.

Now this book is not telling you where to go. This book is reminding you of what you know at a deeper level and who you are at a deeper level. But understand that once you begin to know and understand and operate from your knowing, you have no choice but to face the structures that have been built by society and by your own need for approval and then require yourself to stand in relationship to them to decide what your knowing requires you to do.

If you know that your relationship has a basis in it of approval, you will not want that relationship much anymore. However, you may have the option of transforming yourself in the relationship to the extent that you don't need the approval from your fellows about the person you have chosen to be with.

"I was told I was going to marry a doctor," says the woman who married the doctor because she was supposed to marry the doctor. Now that's an example, but really this goes much, much deeper into your cultural mandates for what is appropriate behavior. And all appropriate behavior is consigned out of the basis of approval.

Paul is sitting here in his chair attuned to a high frequency. He is allowing information through him and he is rendering it through his speech into a recorder and to a human being who transcribes notes. This is not culturally approved-of behavior, if you think about it, but the fact that it is happening is quite miraculous and can benefit many. If the approval standards had been kept, and these informational sessions had not happened, you would be the lesser for it.

So we have given you a very simple example about what happens when someone operates from their knowing or defies the cultural expectation for approval. So you each have these things. And we will go back to the initial idea that we set forth, "I am in my knowing":

> "When I am in my knowing, I will confront those structures or those creations in my life that I have had to be in relationship to. And I will understand very quickly whether or not my relationship to them has truth at its essence, or is created and in relationship to through my requirements for approval."

"You have to get a job." "You have to go to college to succeed." "You have to marry a pretty girl." "You never marry anyone, because that's not right." Whatever your beliefs are, you have to go to them and to begin to experience them, and if they are not resonating with your knowing of your truth, there will be some work to be done. There will be some walls that will be falling down. And as walls fall down, there is much more room for you.

Today we would recommend that you take a piece of paper and a pen and make a list of all of those things that you currently do in your life that you do out of a requirement for external approval. "I look a certain way." "I have a certain job." "I have a certain practice." "I have a certain belief that keeps in alignment with my culture." All of these things will be of benefit to you.

Now it's not like you need to go out with an axe and knock these walls down. The awareness of them, and the belief that you hold around them, will actually support you in changing them. But you cannot do that until you understand them for what they are.

Now this has been very practical information and we congratulate you for your patience, because you really want the energy work. And we have to tell you right now that this is part of the energy work. This is part of the creation of the new consciousness that you are beginning to inhabit, because you can't inhabit the new consciousness to the extent that you are operating from the old paradigms. And what we were discussing right now is a paradigm, and a shift in paradigm from approval to freedom, from ignorance of your actions into knowing what you need from a higher place.

We want to bring you now back to that party. Back to that room where people were standing where there was a need for approval.

When we left you last, you were standing in that room and you were knowing yourself. You did not need the approval of anybody there in the room, but they were needing your approval. Go back to that image and imagine how that would feel. What does it feel like to be the one who knows?

We will now go forward and explain this to you. When you are in your knowing, you are actually in your energy field in a high way. And others around you will experience you this way. But the idea that you could be in your knowing while others cannot brings us back to that belief in separation that we continue to counter in every chapter.

We want you to go back to the room and see yourself as approving of yourself and see yourself as approving of everyone else there, and to be approved of as well. And now we want you to forget about the whole idea. We want you to take the idea of approval out of the equation entirely.

Approval, of course, implies a level of conformity, and to be approved of by others means approving of the standards and requirements for that approval. So why do you even bother engaging in this? That whole room was engaged in behavior that was counterproductive to its growth on an individual and group level.

Approval, the need for approval outside of a teaching tool and outside of a way of gauging behavior on a moment-by-moment level, is actually not very helpful. "I want my teacher to approve of me when I do the math problem right," is actually okay to the extent that it supports you in your learning. But it also creates a pattern of pleasing others so that your own information, and gathering of information, is done to appease an authority figure. Do you understand this? So while there are benefits, you are also placing into practice problems that will have to be contended with in the future.

So we will go back to knowing and we will disband that room with the eager approval seekers once and for all. They don't need to be there. You can be in your knowing without approval.

So let's go back to the exercise that we did yesterday. You were asked to be in your knowing about one thing, one aspect of the self, something that you knew fully—"I know myself as this"—and see what it felt like. Now we will take you to the next step.

"I know myself as an aspect of the Creator." How does that feel? Does that feel completely insane? Does that feel peripheral, as if it's just outside of your understanding? Does that feel false, like it could not possibly be true? What do you know when you encounter that statement? What does it feel like in your frequency to be claiming your knowing as an aspect of

God? What does it feel like to claim your divinity? What does it feel like? What does it feel like? What does it feel like?

What do you mean when you state, "I am Word"? Does it now begin to resonate with you as possibility, or is it a string of words that seems to say it is rendering a conceptual ideal that you have to grapple with?

We are going to get rid of all the language right now for a moment around this relationship and go directly to energy, and go to that speck of gold we went to at the very first chapters: the heart center, and the light within you that exists there.

Imagine again that in the very center of your heart there is a Christ, there is a light, there is a burning, there is a speck of gold. This aspect of the self living between your breasts at the center of your chest is alive and it is well and it is its own consciousness. I want you now, in this heart place, to begin to activate this spark, this piece of light and bring it into alignment with itself as its creation.

"I am Word through my heart center. Word I am Word."

We're withdrawing Paul now.

Ask the heart center now to begin to rise in light. And feel this flame become aligned again to itself at a higher frequency. Let it come, let it come, let it come.

Feel this, please. Feel the warmth at the heart and the radiating heat coming from the light at the heart center. When you feel this, acknowledge it, thank it, and go into relationship with it. Your own knowing exists in this place, and this heat in the heart is the Christ within you. And the heat in the heart that you are beginning to experience is your own light and your own interrelationship with the Christ.

We want you now to allow this light to begin to fill you and to become you. And you don't have to effort this because this light will do the work. Let it come, let it come, let it come.

As the light fills the body, you feel yourself become aligned. And now you allow this light to become you as your frequency. So this light draws to it and embarks on its own journey of expanding around you and enfolding you. Now once you feel this, and you will feel this as an expansion in your field, you affirm this:

"I am Word through my being. Word I am Word.
I am Word through my vibration. Word I am Word.
I am Word through my knowing of myself as Word."

"I am Word through my knowing of myself" is the anchoring of your knowing as a Christed Being. And we are not talking about intellectual knowing. We are talking about your knowing at a vibrational level that will heal you of the

misinformation and the misperceptions and the requirements of approval that you have always engaged in out of
a false belief that you were something other than this light,
other than this aspect of the Creator in consciousness.

And now we bless you with our light. And we want you to
feel your expanded energy field once again and we want you
to feel the light that is now coming to you. We are enfolding
you in our essence, and we are aligning your energy fields to
the vibration of the Christ consciousness.

"I am Word through my understanding of this information
that I am now receiving. I am Word through my creations. I
am Word through all that I see before me. I am Word through
my willingness to know myself as who I am in truth. Word
I am Word through this intention. I am Word. I am Word. I
am Word. So be it."

You have given yourself a present. And you have worked
with your knowing on a level of action. Now this experience
was not just about an expansion of light, it was about an activation of your knowing on a level that you can do at any time
you want. It is not that intellectual, but it is completely experiential. Your light is your light. You are entitled to it. You can
vibrate in it. You sing and dance in it. You can clean the house
in it. But when you are in your light, you are in your frequency
in the higher realms. And you are dedicating yourself through

that information that you acquire to move forward in your knowing and in your growth.

So we give you praise for your industry. And now we will say, we will leave you now at the end of this chapter and continue on to the next one.

Word I am Word.

NINE

TRIALS

March 11, 2009

We want to talk about trials. What trials are, why they come, what they mean, and what you can benefit from them and how you can manage them when they do occur. A trial, in some ways, is an opportunity for rapid growth. And when you call to you a situation that requires you to respond to it in a way that feels like an ordeal, that feels like you have to contend with a trial, you are actually moving forward very quickly if you teach yourself through the process of the ordeal or the trial what the true messages are. Now trials come to everyone. But those of you who embark on a spiritual path may actually call them to you more readily because they present to you the opportunities for growth in a very practical way.

Now Paul always gets frightened around this subject. He doesn't want growth to manifest with trials, he feels he's had enough, and everybody has had enough, really, but they continue when they're required. Now you can always bring your teachings to you in other ways, but your souls will often manifest situations that require you to contend with them rapidly, and these things, we say, can be experienced as a trial.

What a trial really is is a set of circumstances that has been designed to light you up in order for you to dismantle the behaviors that created it to begin with. So if you have a certain kind of crisis in your life, you can put money on the fact that it may have been created by you, at a higher level, to move you beyond those issues that originally created it. We will tell you that when these things happen, your journey has an opportunity to take a jump-start. It really is like you can take a big leap forward.

Now Paul is in the background going, "Can't we take a break? Can't we talk about this tomorrow? I don't really want to go here. It doesn't feel clean to me. Why would Spirit say trials are good?" We are not saying trials are good. Trials are trials, and when they arrive, they must be contended with. We are saying that trials are often created for you and by you to motivate you to change, and trials hold within them promise of wonderful change.

But how you move through them is what we really want to talk about today. How do you move through a crisis? How do you move through a situation that challenges the very beliefs that you are incurring on your spiritual path? How do you make do with information that feels faulty in the face of a trial or a problem of real magnitude? How do you handle your faith when the opportunity for it seems to be presented in such a way that makes you want to run from it, and to leave your faith in the bag by the front door? Where do you go when you get afraid, and how do you handle it?

We will tell you now that when you create a trial, you are actually creating an opportunity for your growth. If you approach the trial as an opportunity for your growth and an opportunity for your learning, you will have a magnificent experience with it to the extent that you don't allow yourself to go into fear. Then it becomes quite wonderful. Imagine, for example, that you were to find out, quite simply, that you were losing your home because you have not paid the mortgage. Now that's a terrible thing for someone to experience on a certain level of consciousness. That requires difficulty, and it also requires magnificent change. Now we will tell you this. We are not recommending this and we are not using this as an example of a good thing to happen, but it is an excellent example of a trial.

So suddenly you are faced in consciousness with a situation that you would fear, and you can go into fear, and you can go into victimhood, or you can go into anger, or you can go into anything, but that's actually not going to sort you through the next stage of the requirement for your growth.

The way to approach this problem, then, on a practical level is you find another place to live, and you understand that your journey is now taking a new formation and you are being replaced in your physical environment in a place where you will learn different kinds of things. The judgment of this situation is what makes it feel like a trial. The attachment to those things that you believed you were supposed to have is what makes this feel like a trial. The belief that someone else has authority over you and where you live is what makes this feel like a trial. The understanding that property is not something that you own, in truth, because it's just matter and can always be changed, is part of the issue you are contending with.

Nobody owns anything, really. Nobody has anything, really, if you think about it. Property is all transitory stuff. It doesn't exist when you are gone in your consciousness outside of memory. That wonderful teacher that you had in first grade who always wore that blue sweater is remembered by her blue sweater, but her blue sweater has long since turned to ash, it has long been gone. And in a hundred years, the magazines that you read and the papers that you value and the paintings that decorate your home will be gone or will be elsewhere. You are borrowing these things, and when you understand the transitional nature of matter, you will understand that you are anchoring your safety to a system of belief that is about owning property and safety and inhabitation of things as opposed to your own consciousness.

Now you are always in your own consciousness. You travel with you where you go.

We are taking Paul out again for a moment.

(Pause)

Okay, we want to talk about what just happened. Paul got worried because suddenly he was dealing with an informational system that challenges his own belief systems. And we are not telling him that it is okay to be evicted; we are only saying that people learn. And what people have to learn is that they are their consciousness and those things that they carry are not their consciousness. They are things that they hold to them and give importance to that ultimately will not be there in a hundred years.

Now we say trials with a real intent for the reader to understand the requirements of herself when she is contending with something like this. And something that challenges one's belief systems must be dealt with in this text. When one is trying very hard to honor the possibility that they are the Christ, what happens when, in the middle of that, you lose your house, or your job, or your marriage collapses or your child is diagnosed with an illness, or you are? How do you contend with this? And that is what this chapter is about and that is why it must be included.

Paul's resistance to this has a great deal to do with his own investment in his own safety. We will give you an example. When a man decides that if he loses his job he will be on the street, he has created a belief system that his job is his safety. When a woman believes that her sense of security and her sense of being and her sense of self-worth is dependent on her husband's presence in her life, she is setting herself up for a huge trial when that marriage dissolves. If you believe that your body cannot handle an illness and will die because you're so frightened of going to the doctor, and you go to the doctor and get the bad news, you have a trial.

Now God is everything, and God is present as a frequency in everything that happens. But to blame God for what happens will not help you right now in the face of the divorce or the loss of work or home or health. We must bring you back into your power and we must align you to your frequency in the Christ, in the reminding of who you are, in order to move you through it.

When you are in this place and you are able to contend with a trial at a high frequency, it becomes a learning experience and nothing more. It becomes an opportunity to create wonderful change. But you must honor the seeds of the new that are present in the old, and you cannot decide in advance that what is on the other side of this trial is going to be worse than what you had. You have all heard stories about people who lose their jobs and then begin to follow their dreams for the first time, or people who leave their spouses or have been left and then suddenly realize a whole other aspect of themselves that has not been present in their experience because they were being overshadowed or controlled by the relationship they were in. You all understand that change holds promise, but you run from it.

Now in most cases, trials present themselves when the need for change and the requirements for change and the mandates for change are such that the whole system needs a shift and the whole being needs to be propelled out of its comfort zone.

This country right now is in a trial, and this trial is presenting itself as cultural magnification of everything that did not work for a very long time. The elements of greed and the elements of ownership and the elements of entitlement are all up for grabs right now as the paradigm shift in this culture is changing.

People believe in this country right now that everything will go back to normal in a year or two and if that were to be the case, that would be a very sad thing. Because this is about transformation and moving forward. And it is not about amassing fortunes and it is not about people being deprived. It is about understanding who you are as consciousness and this country, right now, is having to reidentify itself in its consciousness and therefore is in trial.

The experiences of it, the things that happen to motivate change, are not always kind to the ego self or to the systems that have been created to protect it. So you understand this: When a trial occurs, everything that is encountered is about amassing an energy field that will create change, and that change will then provoke transformation to a higher level if this change is embarked on consciously and not in fear. Do you understand this? Everything can be made new in a positive way if you engage with it as consciousness, and as consciousness we mean, "I am the Word."

"I am Word through that that I see before me."

"I am Word through this situation."

"I am Word through this trial."

"I am Word through what I undergo."

"I am now bringing the light to this situation."

All of these things are in support of monitoring your own consciousness and activating the light in such a way that will support you through these changes.

WE ARE GOING TO TAKE A BREAK NOW. WE WILL resume tomorrow. We will continue with this chapter. We are going to require that you both stop and discuss this for a few

minutes now before we let you go. And then we will take a
break until tomorrow morning. I am Word. I am Word. I am
Word. Thank you both.

March 12, 2009

We're ready for this. And the talk today is about decisions.
Now we are not finished with trials, but we want you to
understand that the decisions that you make when you are in
response to a crisis are the decisions that change the trajectory of your life and path. And most of you move immediately into fear when you are faced with circumstances that
surprise you, unsettle you, and make you believe that your
world is about to be challenged.

   We understand this perfectly and we allow it and we accept
it as your behavior based on your circumstances and your
consciousness, at the level that you are. But, if you will understand that the rate of change that is available to you through
these transformational periods responded to by a crisis can
motivate you wonderfully to the next chapter of your life if
you will allow yourself to respond from a higher perspective.

   When you do this, then you have the opportunity to make
a decision that is warranted and supported by you in consciousness and that is not acting out from a place of trou-
bled fear. "I have lost my home, I have to panic, I have to take
something next. I don't know what it is, but I have to do it

today." "Oh my God, my husband's leaving. I have to save my marriage today." All of these are natural thoughts and the thoughts are fine. We are not talking about your thoughts at this moment. We are talking about the decisions that you make in response to them. Period.

So say you want to make a change and you are frightened of the ramifications of the change based on the situation that you find yourself in. You can stop. You can align your energies to a higher level of frequency and then begin to respond *from your knowing*.

Now we talked about knowing yesterday in the previous chapter for a very real reason. When you are not in your knowing, you are not anywhere to be making a decision from. That is not appropriate. All you can be is in reaction or response. But that is very different from acknowledging the magnitude of ability that you have to know what your requirements are to further your journey forward.

When you do this with the intention to acknowledge your power as a co-creator of your life, you stop being a victim. When you are not a victim, you have choice. When you are in choice, you are in your power and you are not frightened. And the trial, then, becomes a gift of change that is making itself known to you through your circumstances.

Now we are talking about this in a very practical way. We are discussing this as if this is something that happens that you can attend to practically, and we also want to speak about it energetically. And this is a different way of approaching the same issue because, in a funny way, we're going to bypass conscious response for a moment in favor of understanding that you have an opportunity at a frequency level that you can work with as well.

When you are in a situation that you experience as a trial, you go into a survival mechanism because you are frightened, and then your system vibrates at a place of fear and you react until you calm down, or feel better, or things change. That is how things happen when people get shocked and move into fear for whatever reason. Now on a level of consciousnesses you can differentiate between fear and action. You can understand that if you are frightened and you take an action to solve the fear, you can do one of two things. You can move into a higher grace and understand that you are encountering your fear through taking affirmative action, or you can stay in fear and take a fear-based action. And these are two very different things.

If my child is suddenly in big trouble in school, I can work with the problem in a practical way even though I am frightened, or I can respond in fear and take actions to try to control and fix everything so that it goes back to what I thought it was supposed to be. Everybody is always trying to affirm that the way things are is working, and if that child is in serious difficulty in school, you had better believe that there is a real reason for it, and moving forward practically is going to be much more beneficial to the child than trying to fix the problem and put it back where it was. Do you understand this?

So we say to you, when you work with these things consciously, you are working on one level. You are framing it through active experience and consciousness in a practical way. But we can also tell you that to acclimate to the frequency of a situation is a different way in.

Yesterday, Paul was on the telephone with someone who was frightened. He did not need to say what was going on because he felt the energy of fear in his friend's energy field and consequently was able to work with the friend by Wording through the fear to bring the friend back into alignment to the level that he could then move into response. Now Paul is here saying, "Hey, wait a minute, I didn't say anything," and that's absolutely correct. You didn't say anything. You experienced the energy of your friend, you knew what was wrong in frequency, and you attended to it in frequency.

Now we understand that we are speaking of healing another here, but frankly you can attend to your own situations this way as well. So we will say to you this. If you are in a situation that feels like a trial, you have the opportunity to move into the situation energetically and bring the Christ consciousness to the actual situation in frequency.

We will tell you this. When you manifest the Creator in a situation, when you become aware of the presence of the Christ in a situation, the situation is transformed. You understand this metaphorically. We can say, "Yes, I get it," but you don't get it until you get it. And this is what we want you to get. When you understand that the Creator's action, the Word in action, is present in a situation, you can move that situation.

Now please don't believe that we are telling you you can fix something. We just told you this is not about fixing things. "Fixing things" implies that the situation you want to fix needs to be restored to what it was when in fact this is a way of transforming the situation to bring the situation into the higher alignment. Now we are both [P: Who's "both"?] suggesting that this is a mechanism of transformation that will change things when you are willing to align fully to the higher frequencies. We will give you an example.

When you choose to be in a situation for whatever reason, and there is a problem in the situation, calling forth the higher frequency into the situation will align the situation at a higher level. You are bringing the action of the Christ into the situation. When you are doing this, you are transforming a situation. Period. Simply said, it's actually true. You can transform situations through the acclimation and calling forth the Word through that situation that requires change. Period.

Now we will say what we meant by "both," and this is important, Paul, because it threw you. We are working with you, in tandem with your energy frequency. You are gesturing as us, you are imprinting our vocabulary into your own to discuss what's required, so when we talk with you, we are working with you and there is a twosome, you could say, present in this telephone call, in this listening, that we give you from our energies.

Now it is not two people here. You are a "people," if you would, but you are also an energy field. And it is your energy field that is addressed when channel works with you. When our energies are working with you, we assume your energy and we imprint our field into yours in such a way that the manifestation of the required information moves through you readily. You are an instrument that is being tuned, through each transmission, to receive more and more higher attunement so that eventually there will be no resistance in moving through these teachings. You will understand them, and there will not be a pause in your discussions. You will be able to speak more directly. But we say "both." We are guides, we are teachers, we are a collective energy that is transmitting frequency to you on a level of information. You experience this as language or image or feeling, but we are doing the work in tandem with your energy field.

Now everybody who is reading your book, the book that you work with with our frequencies, is also comprised of energy, and they are experiencing this book on multiple levels. This is imperative that this be understood. The conscious mind receives the information and digests it and makes decisions about it. "I understand this." "This is junk." "This is fun." "This is interesting." "I am so surprised." The conscious mind is working with all this information as it responds to this text.

Now on another level, your frequency, the frequency of the reader, is transforming in response to the information that suggests that they are in new shift. And this shift is actually chosen by them through the reading of the book and encountering the energies that the book brings forth.

If you can imagine a jukebox, and every time you play the jukebox you play a different song, and you feel the frequency of the song, and you sing along with the song, and you learn the song, that is all that's happening here. But as you learn the song, your frequency aligns to the song on a higher frequency level. So you are changed by your experience of the song once and for all. That is the message here.

So just as you are being worked with, Paul, as we work through you, the audience of this text is being responded to as well. Now your audience, the readers of this text, need information and that is why this is an informational text. We could just as easily have created a sound that would transmit frequency to attune their energy fields to a light vibration that would allow for resonance. But then that becomes passive engagement. Although the energy field would respond actively to the change, the conscious mind would have a very difficult time understanding what was happening.

So when we said you are being engaged now on multiple

levels, you are idealizing what this means by saying, "I'm being changed." You are being changed, but you are the changer and we are the catalyst for the change as we respond to you, the reader, who is undergoing a remarkable journey in energy shifts and frequency.

So one level is consciousness, one level is intellect, and the other level, finally, is choice. Active soul choice. You cannot do anything without choice. Even when you are being passive and you believe you are being dragged along in your life by the hair, you are choosing that. Do you know this? You are always in choice. Every second of the day, you are in choice.

Now when you understand that your choice is in alignment with the higher frequency and you are in your knowing, the choices that you make are very, very, very different. You do not act on fear. You do not act out of a need for recognition on an ego level. You do not act on a basis of approval seeking anymore. You change the motivations that have informed you, and this is an uncomfortable process. The uncomfortable process is your change. And that is the way you will actually know that you are in this process outside of the shifts you will begin to feel more regularly in your frequency. When you are in the uncomfortability of change, you recognize that you are doing things that no longer serve you. And as you align to the new way of doing it, you shift out of the old and into the new. And this is the process of moving your frequency.

This is not just about retraining your behavior. If you change the behavior but you do not change the consciousness that acts as the catalyst for the behavior, the behavior is really not changed. Paul is seeing the image of someone trying to shimmy into a dress that is twelve sizes too small. And that's really what it's like to pretend that you have a higher consciousness than you really do.

Now we will give you this information. If you are very angry at somebody and you choose not to act on that anger, that is a benefit in many ways to you and to the party you are angry with. However, this is very different than unclogging the blockage that has required you to be in the system of anger to begin with. When you are unclogged, when that pattern that created that anger is no longer in service, you do not act from it because it is not there to act from. The memory of it may exist, but that is quite different than acting on something that is currently operational. Do you understand this?

When you say, "I have changed," and you are not changed, you may be supporting change and affirming change and we support you in that, but that is very, very different than signing a paper with a signature from a new perspective that says, "I am this person. I am not the person I was."

Now this is an example of a manifestation of change: "All of my life I had decided that I had to be a nurse because a nurse is a good person who helps people. And then I go on my journey and realize that my need to help people was based on a fear that if I didn't help people I was a bad person." This does not mean that in your new incarnation you will not be helping people. The Christ that you are in manifestation will be helping people. But you may not want to be a nurse. Or you may realize that you much prefer helping people when it's not out of a place of duty. When it's not out of obligation or a place of feeling "sinful," for lack of a better word.

Those who go to confession believe themselves to be in sin and that is why they go to confession in this religion of Catholicism. Those who do not believe in that process do not engage in it that way. They are not operating from a belief that they need to be forgiven by the man in the booth. That is not who they are, and consequently they don't create their reality from that perspective. So we say to you that the person that they are, once they are transformed, may realize that they are not in sin and that they are already forgiven, and that there is freedom there. But to pretend that you are forgiven, or you believe that when you don't, is false. And that same person might benefit more from the experience of a confessional than he would from denying he still holds that need.

What we are saying to you, really, is that when you transform, you are changed. And the extent that you respond in new ways to your situations and your experiences and your feelings will be the way you understand that this change has indeed transpired. You have changed already through your experience of this text. Your mind has opened and your beliefs have been changed to the extent that you have been receptive to the information.

On a consciousness level of frequency, you have been transformed by the energies that are operating here at a higher level if you have given permission and engaged with the processes that we have suggested. Because they are actually designed to bring you to a higher frequency and to acclimate your field to the Christ vibration, which is, as we have said, what you truly are. Period.

Trials. To go back to the original idea here, the trials that you have faced, responding to the situations that have been created in your life thus far, have been your teachers. We will tell you that you do not continue to need to create them in order to grow, and you have other options. We have to say, though, that when you require these things, they are beneficial. They will keep you in alignment to your higher goals, which may not be what you think they are. If your soul knows that it needs growth, it will find ways of manifesting that growth and then you will have to deal with it on a level of personality to the extent that that is where you still live.

We can talk about practicing unattachment and staying in the moment, but really we believe that those things are as much a by-product of acclimating to the higher frequencies than the way there. If you are pretending to stay in the moment and you are really in tomorrow, you're really in tomorrow. So you might as well understand that to the extent that you become your frequency in an aware way is the way that you can transform your behavior.

Now we would like to give you some exercises to distill this information and chapter in a way that you can work with practically when you encounter situations that perhaps you perceive to be trials. The first thing you need to do is recognize that the situation has the potential to transform your life in a positive way. Once you do this, you release some of the fear that you have attached or would normally attach to the circumstance that you are faced with. The second thing you need to do is make the decision to remain in your power through this cycle or situation of transformation.

Now in order to do this, you're going to need to acclimate to the vibration of the Christ consciousness, and you can do it through this intention:

"I am Word through my intention to acclimate my frequency to the highest level of consciousness available to me, to show me the way through my present circumstance. I affirm that I am being led by my soul's destiny, by my own higher knowing, and by those guides and teachers who would help me as I grow and transform in wonderful ways. I am Word through this intention. Word I am Word."

When you do this, you are bringing frequency to the multiple areas that are inhabiting this problem or situation. You can also bring the energy directly to the situation as follows.

"I set the intention as follows. I am Word through the situation that presents itself to me as an opportunity for change. I affirm that only good will come from this situation and that I am being led through it in a high way towards my perfect destiny. I align the situation to the higher frequencies through this constant affirmation: I am Word through this situation. Word I am Word."

And you can Word through this situation all you wish to. You can Word through your boss. You can Word through the worry. You can Word through the bills and the ability to pay the bills. We are not telling you that this is magic and if you Word through your bills, the bills will vanish. That is not what we are talking about. But what we are saying is that the bills and your relationship to them will move into a different state of consciousness so that you can address them from a place of action or wisdom or knowing and not from fear. Do you understand?

Now the final thing that we want to talk about in response to trials is the idea that you are given your suffering for a reason, and that suffering and pain are your great teachers. They are teachers. We have talked about this already, but when you become attached to pain, you create more pain. And you can do the same thing with a crisis.

You can manifest crisis or a trial, if you wish, for any number of reasons that have nothing to do with your forward motion. You can do it out of fear because you like to be in fear. You can do it for approval, because you think that people will approve of you if you need their help. You can do it for any reason. But if you are in that place, you need to go backwards and go back to the boulder that has created this pattern of crisis, or the need to be in this pattern of crisis, and transmute the pattern with the instructions we gave you in that prior chapter. That will support you. This is a chapter in facing trials that are situational or circumstantial that have been created to forward your advancement as a soul, as a being, as someone engaged in an active process of transforming him or herself into the frequency of Word.

Now we will also tell you that there are things that are created through the acts created in past lives or in a current life that can be referred to as karma. Yes, it is true that there is indeed a balancing that goes forth as you work through your lifetimes. That is not the focus of this text, but we will tell you this. If you decide that a problem has been brought forth in your karmic destiny, you can also decide that it is for your good. So say this:

"I am Word through any situations that come forth in karma in a way that will benefit me fully in my understanding and in my truth. I am Word through the knowledge that my soul's path is a good one, nor do I need to fear that my actions in the past will be brought to me in ways that I cannot handle. I am Word through this intention. Word I am Word."

Now Paul is in the background saying, "Was that accurate? Is that all we're going to say about karma?" We are going to tell you this. You each have karma. You're each working through it. The process of balancing karma is an ongoing one. The acclimation to the frequency of the Word in many ways transforms this, because you are transforming yourself. So when you are moving out of the law of karma, you are moving into the law of the Christ, which means this: You can transform the past through the light, which is very, very different than having to engage with it on a level of karma again and again and again.

So we will say it very simply. When you are in the Christ frequency, you are operating from a different level. You are actually working with a higher frequency that, in many ways, will move through that karma and transform it so that you're not on a battleground with your past actions in repayment or in fear.

We will tell you this. The choices that you make in this

lifetime will be played out not only in this lifetime but the ones to follow. The level of consciousness that you attend to here will be brought forth in your next incarnation. The level of understanding that you acclimate to here will be with you when you return. Everybody is in progress. Everybody is in change. And everybody is in their destiny.

If you can imagine that you are all on a forward path, every man, every woman, every being on this planet is moving forward *regardless of what they may appear to present in form,* you will understand that your destinies are for good. We say that you are all on your way to the Source. Everyone is on their way to the recognition of who they are as an aspect of the Creator. "Word I am Word through my knowing of myself as Word" is stating that. "I am knowing. I am an aspect of the Creator made manifest in form. I am Word through my knowing of myself as Word."

We will connect to you again in a few moments. We would like to take a short pause as we move forward and begin Chapter 10. And the title of the next chapter is "Love Incarnate."

I am Word. I am Word. I am Word. So be it.

TEN

LOVE INCARNATE

March 12, 2009

The decisions that you have made thus far have been beneficial to you, and you are each receiving information at this time that will begin to acclimate to you as you work with it on a daily basis. Understand, please, that you are not in a quick fix here, but you are in the beginning of a process that will continue long after this book has been put down.

We said "Love Incarnate" was going to be the chapter here and we want you to understand what we mean by this. When you are love incarnate, you vibrate at a frequency of love, and we want you to feel what this might be like.

Now Paul is already going, "Whoa, I'm not there yet. How are we gonna do this one?" Well, Paul, you are not the subject of the book and this is going to happen anyway. The vibration of love, when it works through you fully, has powers that will bowl you over. You are this love to the extent that you align to its frequency, and when you are in the energy of love, you are *in love.* To be *in love* means to be in the Creator.

When people tell you they love you, they are probably saying they have a feeling for you, but they may be saying *they love you,* and if they are really saying it, they are holding you in love, they see you as love and they are love incarnate when they are doing that.

When you love someone in a real way, you are incarnating as love. And the love bypasses judgment or criticism and there can be no fear in love.

Now you feel this sometimes, you've experienced it sometimes, but how do you manage it and can you be here for an extended period? Can this be who you are when you are on the breadline, or when you are in the stadium watching the ball game, or when you are alone in your hospital room, or when you are teaching someone, or when you are playing a game? Can you be this love incarnate as you continue on, or is it a momentary experience to be had on occasion when you are prompted by your emotions?

Your emotions are ways that you know yourself. You know how you feel, and you consequently understand yourself based on those responses. And you have partially created your identity in your response to those feelings. "I feel really good when I do this, so I'm gonna do it some more" is actually a healthy response. So we are saying that your feelings are your allies. However, love is not a feeling. Love can be felt, but it is not a feeling. Love is a frequency. It is the action of God expressing himself through you as love.

God's love is unconditional. Understand this, please. It is unconditional. It is manifested as you, as an aspect of you, and if you want to believe that you can experience yourself as love, you can attune to it. But you have to do this through your intentions. So:

"I am now manifesting myself as the energy of love. I am Word through this intention. Word I am Word."

As you manifest yourself as love, your experience begins to transform. And as it transforms, you understand yourself as a vehicle of the Creator in action.

Now we are not going to tell you that you're going to walk around as love when you're cranky, or you're overtired, or you're feeling filthy because you were working in the mud, although you can. We are talking about your frequency again, and when you go into love as frequency, you acclimate to that vibration and then become that. When you love, you are *in love.* When you are *in love,* you are vibrating in the frequency of love. Period.

So you choose this. We have given you the tools in previous chapters to begin to work at this. We have discussed the importance of seeing your fellows as perfect creations. We have discussed the ability that you have to feel frequency and, in doing so, recognize that the separation that exists between you and your brother is only that which is experienced through your own decisions to be separate. We understand that you are in process, and we want you to know that you can claim love and vibrate as love and be love incarnate.

We do not say you walk around laying your hands on people and kissing them because you are so excited *being in love.* That is not what it means. It means that you resonate as love and that your actions then are informed by love. You are the channel of love as you choose it.

Now we want to talk about destiny and the requirement of destiny. And what we mean by this is, as we said in the last chapter, that all souls are moving forward to the Creator regardless of what they present. Paul has heard the anecdote that the bum on the street may have the higher calling in this lifetime than the minister or the doctor. That the bum on the street may actually be learning a lesson in humility that will transform him deeply for lifetimes to come. Now we will not tell you that someone has to be a bum to learn humility, but certainly it is a way forward.

We ask today that you take a walk and that you witness everyone that you pass as in their perfect place in time. We ask that you understand for a moment in time that every man and woman is where they need to be, where they have chosen to be, for the learning that they require, on this day, in this moment. When you understand this, then you will understand that you are the same and we are all in this dance together. And this dance, finally, is in its perfection and cannot be otherwise.

When you understand for a moment that you are right where you are supposed to be in your consciousness and that the circumstances around you are things that you have created to bring you to this place of consciousness, you can then change them. But the perfection that you find in this moment of awareness will be profound. "I am where I am. I see where I am. I am right where I am supposed to be" will liberate you to take change as the miracle that it is. You have opportunities to grow, as does everyone. And you are all where you are supposed to be given what you know, what you have had available to you, and what you have come here to learn.

We will ask you today to make a decision to stay on this path regardless of the resistance that presents itself in the way of your ego, or the manifestations of others' requirements for you.

In the old days there was a great belief in persecution, and a belief that if you embarked on your path in a way that was unique to you, you would be defying a cultural norm and receive punishment through this action. In many of you, the belief that you will be punished if you break out of the norm and you reacquaint yourself with your own abilities as a spiritual being will result in a trial is still present. Many of you, in fact, had experiences in prior lifetimes where you were persecuted for what you believed. So this is an opportunity now, if you wish it, to break through a cycle and patterning that has been imprinted on you out of fear as a way of keeping yourself safe, or out of ridicule, or off the stake and pyre, as it were, in other times. You do not need it again.

The energies that are present on the planet now, believe it or not, are changing everyone. And consequently the level of growth that will be present on this plane in the coming years will be nothing like anything anybody has ever seen. The growth that is present already in your own abilities to acclimate to energy may be surprising you and they will continue to as you continue to work with them.

You say that you are love and then you understand that that is more than a concept, that it is not just an attitude, that it is way of being and operating in a frequency. And in a funny way, that then takes the responsibility away from you on ego level to be love because love is you. So in a funny way, you get out of the way enough to allow love to be love activating and operating and expressing itself through you in perfect ways.

Imagine now that there is one person in your life whom you love deeply. And we want you to see that person before you in your mind's eye. And we want you to hold them in love. We want you to see yourself as that frequency and we want you to see that person before you and then we suggest you set this intention:

"I am Love through the one before me, Love I am Love.
Word I am Word through this intention."

Or you can simply state,

"I am Love through this one I see before me. Word I am
Word."

The intention is the same, see this person and see them
held as love. We are going to suggest, Victoria, that you see
your brother before you, and you see him in love, and you
will see him in spirit acclimating to this vibration and he will
nod his acknowledgment to you, and you will feel this in your
heart. This is important to do today.[2]

So you do this exercise now—"I am Love through the one
before me"—and in doing so, you see the perfection in the
person you see, you hold them in their perfection, "I am Word
through the one before me," and you see them and experience
them in love. "Word I am Word."

Now that was the first step. We would support you now
in seeing someone that you could not stand at some point in
your life standing before you. See them as they were at the time

---

[2] During an interval Victoria had asked the guides about her brother's journey
in life.

you were engaged in difficulty. See that at the time when they were there and present in your life. Stand before them if you wish, or sit where you are, but see them in your mind's eye.

And we say this to you. When you can love this person in fullness, you will be healed of almost everything you can imagine. "I am Word through the one I see before me. Word I am Word." Send the energy to them and let them receive it. You do not have to do anything else at this moment in time. "I am Word through the one I see before me."

Now we are going to ask you this. Are you willing at this moment to hold this person in the frequency of love? What does it feel like? What does it make you feel when you are asked that question? If you can say, "I am willing to try," then we will work with you to take the next step. If you say, "I cannot," we would like you to do this instead:

"I am Word through my willingness to forgive this one I see before me for all things done or experienced by me. I am Word through my knowing that the one before me is a perfect creation of God and I am willing to attune to that truth now. Word I am Word."

That will set in motion the change in consciousness that is required for you to hold this being in love.

Now we will tell you this. To hold this being in love does not require you to go out to dinner with them, nor make a phone call, nor to talk to them about what happened in the past to create the problems. You are working at a consciousness level to heal your relationship with this person on one level, but you are also blessing them in the frequency of Divine Love. "I am Word through the one before me" assumes that they are moving through the energies and frequencies of Word. "I am Love through the one I see before me" brings the action of love, that aspect of the Creator that operates as love, through that being as well.

You may feel this yourself as a warmth through your body. The energy of love feels warm and beautiful as experienced in frequency. And we are not talking about the love you feel from your boyfriend or your cat, but that feels warm, too. We are talking about the frequency of love that you attune to when you say, "I am love."

Now "I am Love through the one before me" allows the love that is moving through you, that is as an aspect of the Creator incarnating as you, to be witnessed and expressed and received by the one you see before you. And if you have someone that you have had difficulties with, and you can truly experience them in love, "I am *in love* with this person," you will then begin to feel the true gifts of the spiritual journey that you are on.

Earlier we said to you, if you could do this, many of your problems would vanish, and we are telling you that that is so. Because when you can achieve this level of consciousness, you can understand fully the level of manifestation that is yours, that is your heritage as a child of God. You are acting as the Creator, and you are loving as the Creator loves, without condition, you are love incarnate. "I love the man who hurt me" is not a personality construct. "I love the one who harmed my possessions," "I love the one who left me behind" or "betrayed me" or "took my things." You can do this through your consciousness.

Understand, please, that the consciousness of the person you are dealing with is also transformed by this action of love. You do not love someone without changing them. Paul teaches. He has students. And his gift as a teacher has always been his ability to love those he teaches in a way that is appropriate to their learning. He sees them as perfect students, engaged in their learning, at whatever level of consciousness and ability they are present for. And in doing that, he witnesses their potential, and in doing that, he is witnessing their divinity. And in witnessing their divinity, they are loved. And that is why people love and are loved and grow when they have that expression gifted to them.

To love someone else in this way requires no return. It does not require beauty, it does not require action on their part, it does not require that you know them or have even heard of them. You can love someone on the other side of the planet as perfectly as you love your brother when you embark on this journey fully and in your awareness as a Christed Being.

You are a young woman in manifestation still. You are

a young man in manifestation still. And what we mean by this is that what is available to you in manifestation will be wondrous to you when you understand that it can be created through your consciousness. What is created in love is eternal. Please understand this. What is created in love is an eternal frequency and the gift of love to another stays with them long after the encounter has gone. You can witness someone in their perfection and transform their consciousness. You can see yourself as perfect and transform your own. When you love someone else in a truthful way, the action of love, the frequency and vibration of love, is who you are. You are love incarnate when you love.

We would like you today to go someplace public, to sit on a bench in a park or a coffee shop or a library or a bus station. It does not matter where you are, but it is important that you do this. We want you to go there and find yourself a nice seat in a corner where you can witness the world before you. And we want you to choose people to love. And you want to do this through your intention. You do not have to speak to them. You do not have to see them face-to-face. The woman walking across the bus station with her suitcase in anticipation of her journey is the one who is deserving of love. The man standing in the corner with the cup begging for change is the one deserving of love. The child with his parent complaining about standing too long is the one deserving of your love. And you will do this:

"I am Love through the one I see before me. Word I am Word."

And in doing this, you will hold this person in the frequency and in the energy of love. We would like you to do this today.

Now we will give you another ambitious exercise, because we've already taken you out of the house:

"I am Word through those I see before me."

We would like you to embrace the frequency of all those before you in the bus station, in the library, on the park bench, in the coffee shop. "I am Word through the ones I see before me." And allow your consciousness then to align to them as a group energy field. You will feel them individually, but you will also feel the energy of the world.

When you do these exercises with frequency, it is extremely important that you understand that you can monitor your own energy field through the systems that you have available to you. And this means your body and your aura, the feelings that you have, what you see, and what you hear. These are things you have available to you.

"I am Word through the one I see before me and I get a headache" may well imply that the person you are tuning in to has a headache. Paul feels what they feel in their bodies to the extent that he is often able to understand what maladies may be presenting themselves in their physical form. You may feel this yourself. "I am Word through that thing I feel," "I am Word through that shoulder," "I am Word through that heart," "I am Word through that bad knee," is all permissible.

As we have said earlier, when you send energy at this frequency, it is not invasive. The energy field of the subject will appropriate the energy and do what is required with it. You are gifting them, you are not fixing them, and there is a huge difference. One is about allowing, one is about controlling, and you do not control this energy, although you can support it in its focus by intending where it is being sent. How it is absorbed and utilized, frankly, is not your business at this stage of understanding. In subsequent texts we will talk more about advanced healing methods, but that is sometime down the road.

Now we will tell you this. If you are Wording through the woman in the coffee shop and suddenly you feel sad, you must understand and let that sadness pass through you. You are not there to absorb and take on empathically energies and problems of others. You can let them pass through you as indications of where the healing is required, but they are not for you to take on. When you take on somebody else's energy in this way, you are not supporting yourself or them. That is very different than working with them through intention to support their healing. So if you feel something empathically, acknowledge it and let the light, let the love, let the frequency do the work.

"I am Word through those I see before me."

The miracle of this, in truth, is that you are beginning to see with eyes of Christ. You are beginning to see and experience the world with the wonder that you have acclimated to and the knowing that you have declared as your divine birthright. As you become love, you become in your awareness a vehicle for the higher frequencies to work with. And you will begin to find that you are led and directed and supported in those things that you need to do to support you, and this wonderful work will be made clear to you.

This does not mean that you are doing this work professionally. It may mean that you are riding in an elevator with someone who requires the light, or that you are teaching a student who, one day, will break through in consciousness in a way that will transform the planet, and you will have given him permission on an energetic level to remember who he is in frequency.

You do not have to know what the benefits of the work will be in order to do it. In a funny way, it's not your business. "I am Word through those before me." You became a witness and an active part of every situation you are in, because you are the vibration of the Word and you are acting it through your intention to serve. "I am Word through those before me." What you do is you bring energy to everyone there. You are not depleted because, as we have told you, you are the conduit, you are the vessel that the divine frequency inhabits, is, and works through:

"I Am that I Am. I Am that I Am. I Am that I Am."

That is what you are, in truth. You are that you are. Word I am Word.

Now we want to take a moment and talk about the next chapters. And the next chapters are very important. One is about creation and one is an epilogue. We will discuss them both tomorrow, and on Saturday we would like to complete this, and we would finish it with a blessing and a seal that the readers may be receiving this text in perfect form, through the perfect person and publisher who will manifest it. This must be created and must happen, in the perfect way.

This is not a vehicle for monetary gain. This is a vehicle of transformation. And we would like you to benefit from the work you are doing; however, the work that you are doing is really meant to benefit the reader. You both are present through this channeling to attune yourselves and to gift yourself with the knowledge that you need to fully, truthfully reclaim yourselves as you are. "I am Word" is the declaration we have given you, and we thank you both today for your time and for your energies. Word I am Word.

Stop now, please.

ELEVEN

CREATION

March 13, 2009

We're ready for the talk. And today was creation. Today is the day we discuss the manifestations of the work you have done to date. Now Victoria has already told you that she has had an experience in consciousness that reclaimed her understanding about the limitlessness of time.[3] And that's as good a way in to this discussion as any.

You all have constructs that you have worked with in your life that you agree on and partake in on a daily basis. The clock strikes two, so it must be two. The weather is cold, so I must wear my sweater. You have these conditions that you have all agreed upon and you acclimate to and they become a shared truth. Now the truth that you are sharing, believe it

---

[3] The previous afternoon Victoria had an experience of past and present time happening simultaneously.

or not, has been created by you on a complex level of thought and intention that has been imbedded for many, many, many, many lifetimes on a collective level. You have all done this. The world that you exist in is an out-picturing of your requirements for a world that you need to live in.

Now we will tell you this once. This was created by you in tandem with consciousness and the Creator. It can be recreated again and again and again. Now time, we will tell you, is a construct that you agree upon. You agree upon this in many, many ways. Now we are not going to tell you to throw out your watches or your calendars. They are very handy. When we began this experience of channeling this text, we required that Paul and Victoria set a time daily to meet so that we could be present and that the work could commence in a disciplined way. This was appropriate.

Time has its function. Time has its reality as a construct that can be worked with. If we were to tell you now that you could travel in consciousness to a thousand years in the future and witness the events that would be happening there, you would be astonished.

But we would also tell you this. It's happening now. In a thousand years you are still sitting here in this chair speaking these words. And you are elsewhere and elsewhere and elsewhere. Dimensional understanding is a vast science that we cannot even begin to bring you to in this text. However, we will tell you this much. The construct of time is flexible to the extent that you create through your consciousness with an understanding that time is flexible. When you believe that everything happens now, everything can be healed now. Everything is happening now. There is no other time. There never has been. There never will be. It is now, it is now, it is now.

Now you are in a creation that is the physical form that you exist in, and this physical form will die one day. That is a promise. Your physical form will have outstayed its welcome and you will move on into another consciousness frequency without this body. And then one day you will claim another one, and you will ascend again in consciousness to the frequency that you can hold in that lifetime and in that framework and through the construct that you exist in.

Bodies are vehicles of consciousness and nothing more. They are fun, they are wonderful, they are gifts, but they are the vehicles of consciousness. Consciousness extends beyond the body and consciousness extends beyond the construct of time. There is a reason that Paul can feel what is happening in the energy system of Victoria's cat. The cat is present in Paul's time, and time, at this level, does not exist in the same way on the same clock. Everybody is in frequency. Frequency has rules. But the rules that frequency has do not exist in the same constructs or dimensional frameworks as physical form.

You understand this already in some ways. When you dream, you depart the body and you have another experience of consciousness where one moment you are in a hallway and one moment you are in a tree and one moment you are having a conversation with a dead relative. All of this is happening at the same time. In the other realm you are not restricted by the vibrations of the denser energies that require you to stay in your chair and walk down the street. People fly in dreams all the time, and guess what? They are flying. They are unmoored from the limitations of the frequency of the physical plane.

Now your consciousness, being who you are in truth, is always unlimited by matter in this way. Paul had a discussion yesterday with a man who said, "I just want to leave my physical form." And we said, "The physical form is where this needs to happen in." And we want to explain what we meant.

People, throughout time, who have engaged in deep spiritual work have disguised self-loathing of the physical body or physical experience with a desire to attune to the higher realms. People have used spiritual growth as a way of escaping their issues or their pain. Convents have been requiems for many, many years for people who did not need to engage in physical reality but preferred a life of contemplation and the mind, and that is fine. However, we are telling you now that the vibration that you are anchoring in is in physical form, which means only that your experience of it, your experience of higher dimensional reality and frequency, will be experienced through the physical form that you exist in.

Now this is a big thing. You don't have to meditate and float off in consciousness to access information. Now Paul was wondering, "Why? Why did it take so long for someone to receive enlightenment and why were the paths always so arduous for the seeker?" The answer again is in the manifestation of frequency on this plane. The density of matter and vibration was such that in order to move through it, you had to work hard. You had to work very hard. And you had to have a lot of help in the higher realms to break through the density of frequency. That is not the case now. The frequency on this plane has shifted and this is allowing you to lift. You are part of the lifting.

Paul gets an image that we would like to describe. He is seeing people swimming through mud, attempting to get through muddy water to break through the surface to be in the light. And we will tell you this. In some ways, that is an accurate description of the trials that face the seeker in the denser energies. But the energy now is much clearer and the rise is not effortful in the same way. However, because the rise to the light, to the service, is required through choice, what you have to make do with is the reality that you are the one choosing this journey. And when you do, you have to confront those things that impede your growth. You can say, if you wish to extend the metaphor, that those are things that you bump into while you are swimming to the surface. But if you understand that they can be moved and that your path can continue upwards without real obstruction, you will understand the journey and the great mystery that is being revealed to you through the process of engagement with this text. This is a manifestation of the Christ consciousness inhabited in man. This is the gift of consciousness of the Christ frequency manifested in man. This is a big deal.

Now we tell you "big deal" in the way that we do so you don't get silly. There are many people who still believe that spiritual growth is about feeling nice and painting pictures of rainbows. Or they feel that it is about suffering and crawling on their knees to an altar over broken glass. People believe these things because it is convenient to them and it is convenient and ascribes to their heritage and their history. It's what they were taught, it's what they believe, and consequently it is what they will create. So creating anew is the process of this text. We are giving you support in a way of ascending in frequency and consciousness through the activation and wonder, wonder of the Word.

Now the Word is the gift of God that was incarnated as the Christ many times in the history of this plane. And we will sing it to you now in frequency if you wish to receive it as a song in frequency:

The Christ has come again in man! This is the time! This is the time! This is the time!

And you are the vehicles of this manifestation to the extent that you align to the gift that is being given to you. You are the first in a generation of conscious beings coming into form and you will make it possible for those that follow to exist more easily in the higher frequencies that are now available. This is a gift, but this is a massive change. It's a tidal wave of light ascending into you as you ascend into it. You are all rising. Everything rises to the light of the Christ consciousness now. This is promised.

So we said the chapter was "Creation." We have spoken to you about time and the elasticity of time and the fact that time is a creation of man that has been required for him to organize his experience in a consensual way, so everyone can have the same date on the calendar and agree to show up for work. Simply said, that is all it is.

Time actually moves much beyond the structures that you have imposed on it. But for our purposes in this writing and transcription, we will say to you this. Your experience of time can change today only in that you can realize that it is a limitation and nothing more. When you ascribe to the belief that you are free of time in a real way, you align to the next level of frequency. And the reason of this fact is, simply put, you have limitlessness at your fingertips, and you decide, quite simply, that that is accessible to you, and suddenly you can begin to experience anew.

Paul was saying yesterday to someone that so much of this seemed to him to be about permission. Permission to understand, permission to ascribe to a set of beliefs that you already know but haven't believed you had the right to, permission to ascend, permission to forgive, to be forgiven, and to align to the consciousness that you truly are. And permission is truthful, that's a good way to say it. But the permission is only the key in the lock. When the door opens fully, the light pours through you and you become one with the power that created you in consciousness. This is the gift.

Now to ascribe to time gives you limitations. And you're already asking yourself, "I see this on the page, it's very interesting, I don't trust it. When, when, when will I have this experience that is promised to me?"

The moment you say, "Yes." The moment you say, "Yes." The moment you say, "Yes." We will say it again. The moment you say, "Yes," with your soul, with your consciousness, with your being, with your consciousness as the vibration of Word.

"WELL, I'M NOT THERE YET," IS YOUR RESPONSE. DO you want to be? is our request to you. Do you want to be? Do you want to be on this path? If you do, you are worked with by us. The higher energies are available for this work on a level of sponsorship and it is availed to you now, any moment you request it, through this intention:

> "I request that I am being served with the information and with the energies required for my shift in consciousness. I am Word through this intention. Word I am Word."

When you state this intention in truth, which means you believe it, you call to you the frequencies that you require. Now how much faith is necessary? The size of a mustard seed has been said, and that is very true. You have enough faith to continue reading this book in the promise that you may understand. And we say to you, we give you the promise back that if you believe that we are requesting you to align to the Christ consciousness, we would not leave you beside the doorway and not invite you in to the great party that is in progress.

All men and women are called to this time to wonder, to believe, to experience. And we say you have been called, you have been brought here to this altar, and on this altar you divest the things that have been keeping you in misery and in separation. And on this altar you rise, you rise, and you sing a new expression, "I am Word!"

And through this expression you co-resonate with the energies of creation, in God's light and in the sound and in the song of love. We offer this to you in parting, because this

book will be gone soon in transmission, that the energies of
the Lord are present now, in this moment in time, and everyone, everyone, everyone is benefited by this the moment they
say, "Yes! Yes! I am Word."

We have called you here to this experience, to the creation
of this text manifesting daily over a period of days through
the missive that we have titled *I Am the Word*. We will tell
you that this was an instructional text that has been ascribed
to you for your growth, for your learning, and through your
willingness to receive it.

This book was channeled in response to your request.
We have come here with this information because you have
asked for it, not because we demand it of you, but because
you have required it from us in a higher level. You have said,
"I am willing to grow and I don't know how. I want to believe,
but I don't see the way. And I want to learn, but I get confused
because everything seems so weighted by ritual, or by fear, or
by my mother's beliefs, or my brother's, or my culture's."

Now we have said to you that we have brought this book
forth for a reason. And we have also said that this information
will be shared through other mediums in other cultures in a
language that is appropriate to them.

We do not deny any God that is a true God. And any God
that is a true God is the One God with another face appealing
to a section of people who have been raised to witness that
God, but they are all one energy.

Everything, finally, is the frequency of light. Everything. And the manifestation of Christ within man, which is the work of this book, will be manifested throughout all men in time. Get over any belief now that this is the province of the Christian or the Jew any more than it is the Muslim or the Hindu or the Buddhist. To do that keeps you back in your ego and in your special-ness. This is appropriate text for this culture, and the frequency of the Christ knows no title and knows no language but truth.

Understand this. The Christ within you is the truth of who you are in essence, and the manifestation of the truth of who you are in essence is the creation of wonder and God within you realizing Himself through your experience of you.

God bless you each as you journey forward. This has been an exciting experience for us to be able to give you this teaching. We are blessed in your creations. You must create the Word through your intention to resolve to become this light in choice.

"*I am Word through my being. Word I am Word.*

I am Word through my Christ consciousness. Word I am Word.

I am Word through my frequency. Word I am Word.

I am Word through my knowing of myself as Word."

We will continue this text now with a message for each man and woman who wishes to praise the Creator.

We would like you now to take a moment in silence and to "be still and know that I am God." And to say that means to move into your own heart and receive the blessing of the Christ at an energetic level, at a level of frequency. We bring your heart now to light and we align to the flame within you, and that flame is the Christ in manifestation in the heart of man. And we allow this flame to begin to move through you and envelop you, in beauty and in fullness. "I am the Word." Know yourself, please. And know that part of the you that is the Creator seeking to know himself, to experience himself, and know you in this light. Word I am Word. So be it.

Addendum

We will end the book tomorrow with an epilogue, which will be slightly different. It will be about your experiences to come, and about the message of the book and the vocation of the reader to bring this energy forth on a daily basis and to work with it fully in matter. That is important. The teaching of this book, in present time, has completed, only to the extent that it has come to a close in terms of the lectures. Tomorrow will be discussion, it will be amplification of the ideas already addressed, and it will be about the practical application of the work that is to come.

We have said to you already, Paul, that this is the first in three texts. And this is the mission text. This is the text that offers the call, and the response to the call will be the next two texts that we will scribe through you when it is appropriate and when you are willing to sit quietly and learn.

The following texts will be quite different. They will not draw on you as a character, nor will they assume you have any information on the subjects that you speak of prior to engaging with it. For this to occur, you have to become a cleaner channel, which means you must channel directly, and that will have to come through your willingness, through your belief, and through the identification of the Christ consciousness that is the teaching of this book.

When you understand that you are, in fact, aligned to the Christ consciousness, that it is not just an ideal to be worked towards, you vibrate at that frequency. When you are vibrating at that frequency, we can work through you very directly. Right now we work through you very well, and we are grateful for the instrument that is your energy system, and we are grateful for the imagination that you were born with that allowed you to believe that this could even be possible.

But we gift you now with the frequency that will bring this lecture to the next level of informational action. And

that means you need to become the passive frequency that
we operate through you in order to bring forth the Science of
Light, and the Christ consciousness. We will be talking about
healing, we will be talking about knowledge, and we will be
talking about other realities in ways that you do not assume
to have any information on, because guess what, Paul? You
really don't, other than what you have intuited through our
infrequent discussions and mentions of such things. So we
thank you both for your attentiveness.

Paul is asking, "Is this part of the text?" and we will say it
may be an addendum to the last chapter on creation, but it
is not a chapter in itself. This is instruction, and this is about
benefiting from knowledge about where we are taking you.

We bless you, thank you. Word I am Word. Goodnight.

EPILOGUE

March 14, 2009

The responsibility of the book you have written and we have written with you is of its own accord. What this really means is the book has its own life, this text has its own correction to make before it goes out into the world. And this text will be received by those who require it.

We want to talk for a few minutes about the corrections we would like to see made in this text before it is sent to the world. They are very, very few, but they are important. The mission of this text was to accomplish a vibrational frequency alignment to the reader, and that has been connected to words on a page on one level, and the intention of the book on another. And we say "your book" only in that you are the transcriber of the information and that will happen in its own accord.

However, our book, the real book, is happening on a frequency level, and our corrections to this text are to ensure that the information acclimates itself appropriately to the frequency that we require to dismantle the frequencies of fear and judgment that will surround this text for several decades to come. Now we say decades, because this is going to be a text that is going to be considered a seminal work in a vibrational chapter that this country is beginning to embark on in their understanding. There is vibrational medicine, there is much happening by way of consciousness that understands things like, "You think something and then you manifest," and this is going to be one piece of a larger canon of work. However, when we say two decades, it's going to take that long for the recognition of the value of this work to move past the frequency of fear that says man is not allowed to be the Christ in form. So we have to address this now. And when we say corrections, we want to go through the text one time with a fine-tooth comb with Paul as the eyes and Victoria as the listener and see what has to change.

Now this is done as follows. No, it is not about editing, it's about hearing. Paul, when you work through this text, typing it from the tapes, you must allow our intrusion. As we say, "This must be corrected," you will understand automatically what we are telling you. You will not have to change more than a word here and there, and the word will be changed because you heard the wrong word the first time. It will be as simply stated as "mouse" changes to "mice" or "house" changes to "hose." It's that kind of a change. But understand this, these are frequency changes.

When the text aligns in appropriateness to the frequency it's intended to be, the transformational powers are significant. So we are really just ironing out the wrinkles so this can be recognized on a causal level by the light bodies, by the consciousness of the readers, so that they will appropriately acclimate to the properties that we bring forth in frequency. So that is one thing.

Now Paul is saying, "Okay, so I write with a typewriter and I say, 'Is this right?'" No, no, no. We will interrupt the transmissions and say, "This must be corrected." You can mark them in the text from the original text with an asterisk to state this has been changed in revision, if you wish, but we would prefer that the few words that we feel are awkward be transposed on the page so that the reader has the true experience that is intended for them.

Now Victoria's role in this is as listener, and it has to do with the authenticity of listening. "And if I choose to listen as the reader, what is my experience?" Now for Victoria, this means she has been a receptive party to a series of lectures on the evolution of consciousness, and we are grateful for her attentiveness. And as a result of her attentiveness, she has already begun to shift her frequency in ways that are palpable to her. She will have to continue this on her own with her own intention, because this book is a discipline, as we have stated. The exercises therein are things that need to be addressed, and in fact the tools are present on a level of consciousness, not only in the writing but in the intent of the book to anchor you in the frequency of the Divine Light of the Christ presence. So that is available to you.

However, when we tell you that your process in the engagement of this book will now become a little more active, we mean it as follows: Victoria needs to receive the information of this text on an auditory level again in order to play this through her consciousness. No, Paul, this does not mean that she has to listen to all the cassettes, that's not what we are saying. What we are saying is that when she reads the text, she needs to hear it aloud in her consciousness and make notes where she is understanding and not understanding. It's a very simple process of annotating a text with questions.

Now these are not questions that are going to be answered in the current text. We will not take the time here to do that kind of work. However, what you may find is that these questions begin to resonate and will be addressed in another book in a very direct way.

Now we said already that this is the first text of three and the other two texts are very, very different because they are not personal in the same regard. Paul has been a character here, and Victoria has been addressed as a listener here in very direct ways, and this was for a reason. You are both actually teaching this frequency in time. Paul, you do it in your groups now, but Victoria, believe it or not, as she aligns to this frequency will have opportunities as well to resonate and teach the Word in vibration. And she will do this in her writing and in the teaching that she does. This is actually her choice, but she will find that her brain cannot stop thinking about this, and the only way to address it is to record it and to act upon it in accordance with the teachings that she has received.

Now this is a privilege to the extent that you wish to engage with it. It does not bypass the intellect at all, but what it does do is reclaim the intellect into its appropriate place in consciousnesses. And in order for that to happen, Victoria will find that her experience begins to change. When intellect is replaced by knowing, there is confusion and disorientation on a temporary level as one thing is displaced in favor of another. So if you understand very simply that you stand on a subway that is rocking a bit, just hold the handle and trust that you are steady and will not fall over. The train pulls into the station and there's a new wonderful vista available to the seer when she emerges from this piece of the passage.

Now the book itself, when it is published, and we do say we intend this to be seen, will have some recognition that you will both have to encounter. And this means to be in alignment with your roles in the creation of this text.

For Paul, it means he has to understand that his work will become visible, and he has been frightened of that for more than twenty years. He has believed on a certain level that if he is seen for who he is, something terrible could happen. This is actually a past life creation. It's old stuff, it needs to clear and it has already, to the extent that he has been allowing himself to be used at this level in accordance with his Higher Self and his willingness to serve as a teacher and as a vehicle for these transmissions. So he is having to contend with some of that now, and this will exacerbate once this sees print. He has to know right now that he is completely protected through this process. He has work to do still, and we would not have him run for the hills the moment somebody said, "This is strange, this is very strange." And that's going to be said by people who are not at a place of readiness to establish themselves in the next phase of their consciousness through the acclimation to Word.

Now in Victoria's case, her role has been quite different. She has been the seeker who came upon the Rosetta Stone and will spend some time understanding what the symbols mean. Now there are two ways for you, Victoria, to associate your role in the creation of this text. You have been the listener, you have been the required witness, and we would actually recommend that you write a very brief foreword to this text that discusses your discovery of and your engagement of this information. What you are actually doing by doing this is giving the permission to the reader to say, "I am entering as well into an understanding that I may not have had previously. I am willing to understand as I go on and have this experience."

In Paul's case, he should write a very brief preface that discusses his ability to hear. And how that was appropriated through this text will be understood as he is discussed. When they say, "What is he hearing?" we will say, "What he is hearing is this book in form."

Now the two of you are going to do this again to the extent that you align to this as a process and you must become comfortable with this as a form of discussion. And this is what this book is, in many ways—a form of discussion. This is an oral teaching that is being transcribed verbatim and translated on the page for the reader. We said corrections, and we remind you that the only corrections we will support are text changes that we say were originally misheard and mistranscribed. And ultimately you will understand, Paul, that your role as channel is to hear accurately and then render accurately what you are being told. This happens already now and it's going to get a lot stronger as the channel is opened.

Now people are going to be receiving information through this text that is going to inspire them to act, and this is important to understand: that the response of the reader to this text is her own responsibility. We work with people to support them in their growth, but we do not take responsibility for someone who runs with the information based on their own fears, their own sense of entitlement, or their own sense of specialness. It's not a lot different than saying, "Guess what, everybody, here's the ticket to Rome," and suddenly someone says, "I am going to Rome to be the Pope." And that is a fun example for Victoria.[4]

Guess what, everybody? There are no more popes. There aren't any in this text. You are all equal in relationship to the vibration of the Christ. That is the great truth. So if somebody elects to use this information in a way that supports special-ness, we say to them now, you are misinterpreting the message of this book.

This is a book about claiming the truth of who you are in light. And light is the one thing that is shared by all. You are all created in the image and likeness of God and just because somebody seems to say that they know more does not mean that they do. Because somebody says that they are of a higher frequency does not mean that they are. So you must stay humble to your own recognition that you are a vessel of the divine. To the extent that you do that, your journey is clear. When you misinterpret this text and you go forward

---

[4] Victoria had a dream the night before that she was being required to travel with the Pope as an attendant and she was unsure what the right protocol would be.

on a mission to do something that is actually in gratification of your ego, you actually dismantle the structure that we are trying to build, and that is a building of light.

Now we are congratulating each of you that you have been aligned to this text to align the self to the Christ vibration. That you have seen this journey through to the final page. And we want to give you some recommendations about how to work with this energy on a practical level in your daily practice. Every day we would recommend that you set this intention:

"I am Word through all that I see before me. Word I am Word. I am Word through the knowing that I need to understand, to receive, to know the intentions that I must set to serve my highest good and greatest growth. I am learning, I am learning, I am learning."

We will tell you each that your methods of transformation may be the same, but your experiences are going to be remarkably different. As you move forward on a daily basis, you begin to understand the shifts that are coming at you through your experience of your energies and your perceptions of yourself and others. Once you regard yourself as a Divine Being, "I am Word, I am Word, I am Word," once you do this on a conscious level, you are acknowledging your divinity as the son, as the daughter, as the vehicle of the Christ message.

Now we say to you this. As this happens, your knowing transforms, and what has not felt truthful in the past will become very uncomfortable, and as that is dismantled, you have to be willing to release preconceptions about who and what you are in a stable way. And we say stable because we are not telling you that you are going to fall apart as a result of having engaged with this text any more than you would fall apart if you read a scripture, or a novel, or a cookbook.

This is actually a text that is understood by you on multiple levels, consciously, unconsciously, and in your frequency. Your Higher Self is aligning yourself to this information and making this journey for you in a way that is appropriate to you. And you must understand that your experience will then be reflected at you in a way that is most appropriate for your learning.

If you have a karmic lesson to learn in this lifetime, you can believe that that lesson will come to you in the way that is appropriate to you. The same is true with this text. This text is the catalyst for your own experience of your own divinity and the divinity of others. That is this text. And as you engage it, you have to remove the blocks that have kept you from this awareness that is ever present in truth.

On a soul level you know what you are, you know who you are, and you know who your brother is. So you don't have to fear this. All you are letting go of is that which vibrates at a lower frequency that you have outgrown. You are shedding skins. And while that may be strange, it does not have to change your level of safety and agreement that you are in your world and you are moving forward in ways that are truthful to you. Now we tell you each in way of understanding you and your needs that there is an alignment now on this planet that makes these things possible and will continue to do so.

Now Paul is wondering again about the resistance to the text. And actually, Paul, this is your own fear projecting into the future, about what could happen and would there be judgment and would it be perceived as a manifestation of something other than the Christ. We will tell you this. The work of the book is in its own light. This book has its own frequency, it has its own readership, it has its own mission, and this has been intended before you were decided on as the vehicle for the message. So we will tell you this. You have to let it go and be what it wants to be. Many will be blessed, many will be frustrated. Many will learn, many will wait to learn. Many will be outraged and many will be delighted. But all of them who engage with this text will become realized one day at one time when it is appropriate for them to do this on their level of consciousness.

That does not mean that the woman who throws the book across the room after page three is going to get the message of the book. That may take some time. But we have said to you already, everybody is changing. The planet is vibrating at a different frequency. The light is here. Everybody is having to acclimate. This is a book of instructions and allowances and intentions that will support you in acclimating to this frequency and working with it in a conscious way. It's not a lot different than knowing that you are in a storm as opposed to just experiencing and not knowing what kind of storm you're in. And we don't use storm in a way that implies discomfort. It's just a graphic image that you can work with that supports the idea that you are in change and everything around you is in change as well.

We like this metaphor enough to give you an example. You go to bed one night and you wake up and there is a blizzard out your window and everything is obscured and it looks slippery on the street and there's a lot of stuff going on. And the cars move slowly and you don't know what to wear because you had not prepared for a storm. But a day later, you walk out of your home into a wonderland of light, and you step in the snow and you are wonderfully surprised at the beauty that has come while you were hiding in your house wondering what was going on outside. In many ways, this is what you are each undergoing. The storm is present, it's going to be a knockout when it quiets down, but as you move through it, you might as well get an understanding of how to navigate the new landscape that is making itself present.

Criticism will be an issue not only for this person who sits here with a tape beside him and a telephone at his side, dictating this information to the woman in California who writes furiously so she does not miss anything. This will happen. And guess what, both of you? It will not be significant to your experience, so you do not have to fear. But we will advise you to stay strong in your own willingness to engage on your own path.

You have to remember that you are the students of this book as much as anybody else is. We are working through Paul's system. We are working through other systems of other mediums and channels at this time as well to support this information in reaching the people that it is intended for. And we are blessed by the availability of this service, just as the reader will be. But we recommend to you now that you never forget that God is the Creator and you are in service to the Creator through your actions, through your availability, and through your willingness to be of service. We are understanding you as the Christ made manifest, as we are understanding all men to be.

Now understand this, Victoria. You had an issue yesterday about language, and you asked if our language was archaic. Our language is not archaic. However, it is translated for Paul and we use some of his vocabulary that we have appropriated in ways that gives us permission to approach a reader at a more modern level. But our language is our language, and we choose our words very carefully. And we would advise you that the use of the word "man" is the appropriate word to address the reader here. All men, regardless of their gender, are in transformation, and if you can understand that, the duality of sex and pronouns and all of those things can actually be obscuring of a real truth. We do not want to argue, but we will say that it is truthful to use this word in this text at this time. Man is the creation of God and that is why we use this word. It does not provide a distinction between appropriate pronouns. It does not describe men or women in body. It is the word we have been gifted to offer you in this text.

Now Paul is wondering, "Does all of this information belong in a chapter?" Much of it feels personal to these two people who we are talking to. Well, we will tell you this. This is an epilogue, this is the finishing, and we have said to you yesterday there would be a seal opening up in consciousness at this time. And we will do this now.

We are now setting the intention for all of the readers of this book, that as they are being shepherded in their higher realms' attention to their growth, we are affirming in consciousness that they are being supported in their acclimation to the Christ frequency, and we now align our energies to them to support them in the realization of themselves as the Christed Self they truly are. We give permission to each man and woman who undertakes this journey to realize herself, himself, in the frequency and in the vibration of the Word. And we join you now in your efforts to align to the new light that is available to you. I am Word through this intention for the reader. Word I am Word. So be it.

We congratulate you both for your attentiveness to this process and we thank the reader for engaging with us so fully. We leave you with blessings. We leave you with Christ and we leave you with this:

I am Word.

ACKNOWLEDGMENTS

Tim Chambers, Jeffrey Kripal, Mitch Horowitz, Jeannette
Meek, Victoria Nelson, Michael Murphy and the Esalen
Institute, and the members of the Thursday Night Energy
Group.

ABOUT THE AUTHOR

Paul Selig was born in New York City. He attended New York University and received his master's degree from Yale. He had a spiritual experience in 1987 that left him clairvoyant. As a way to gain a context for what he was beginning to experience, he studied a form of energy healing, working at Marianne Williamson's Manhattan Center for Living and in private practice. He began to "hear" for his clients, and much of Paul's work now is as a clairaudient, channel, and empath. Paul has led channeled energy groups in New York City for many years. Also a noted playwright, he teaches at New York University and is the director of the MFA in Creative Writing Program at Goddard College. His website is www.guidedreadings.com.

If you enjoyed this book, visit

www.tarcherbooks.com

and sign up for Tarcher's e-newsletter to receive special offers, giveaway promotions, and information on hot upcoming releases.

TARCHER
PENGUIN

Great Lives Begin with Great Ideas

Connect with the Tarcher Community

• • •

Stay in touch with favorite authors
Enter weekly contests
Read exclusive excerpts!
Voice your opinions!

Follow us

 Tarcher Books

@TarcherBooks

If you would like to place a bulk order
of this book, call 1-800-847-5515.